Julius D. J. Erving

Clemon Johnson
#45

#4

Earl
25
Cureton

#31
76ers

Maurice
Cheeks

We Owed You One!

By Pat Williams
THE GINGERBREAD MAN
THE POWER WITHIN YOU

By Bill Lyon
THE WORLD OF SPORTS

We Owed You One!

The Uphill Struggle of the Philadelphia 76ers

Pat Williams and Bill Lyon

TriMark Publishing Company, Inc.
Wilmington, Delaware

ISBN: 0-914663-00-3

Contents

A Tribute From President Ronald Reagan

The White House: With your dogged determination, your high style, your fierce competitiveness and your great talent, you've given new meaning to the "Spirit of '76."

You came so close to winning the championship so many times before, others have become frustrated. But none of you gave up . . . I know that "Dr. J" and Moses Malone are two of your brightest stars, but it took every one of you pulling together to make this dream come true.

Your regular season was nothing but awesome . . . and your performance in the playoffs set a new NBA record. I think Coach Riley of the Lakers put it best when he likened your playoff style to "controlled fury." And he should know, since he was on the receiving end.

But whenever people excel the way you have, it's usually because they burn for excellence somewhere down deep inside. I remember once reading that "Dr. J" said he put the most pressure on himself because of his ambitions to be the best basketball player ever. "What happens around me," he said, "can't put any more pressure on me than that."

Well, your team history of come-from-behind striving tells me that you felt that internal pressure as a team. You were determined to be the best, and, because of that, today you are. I can't think of a better example of the American dream come true.

June 8, 1983

We Owed You One!

The Rainbow Chasers:
An Introduction

9-73

That is not a date. It is not a measurement. It is not a formula or a combination or part of a zip code or a phone number.

It is the won-loss record of a basketball team; specifically, the Philadelphia 76ers of 1972-73.

The 9 and 73ers, they were called. A hot streak was when they had back-to-back days off. They lost their first 15 games of that season. And then, when they finally won their first game, their coach, Roy Rubin, celebrated by icing down his leg. He had jumped up to dispute a referee's call during the game, and had jumped so violently that he pulled a muscle. That's when you know things are going bad.

They got worse.

They got so bad that even players refused to join the team, saying they would quit the sport entirely rather than play in Philadelphia. For example, Marvin Barnes, who had been an All-American at Providence, was drafted by the Sixers and was so horrified at the prospect that he said: "I'll go work in a factory first."

The team did a little better the next season. A little, but not much. They only lost 57 games out of 82.

The only basketball teams that seemed to lose as often as the Sixers were those squads that played the Harlem Globetrotters, and at least they had an excuse: they were *paid* to lose.

All of this forlorn history is dredged up here not for the sake of cruelty, but to give you a perspective. To appreciate how far the 76ers have come, it is necessary to realize just how far they had to travel. For victory is never so sweet unless it has been preceded by failure.

What follows is the story of a group of people whom the authors have chosen to call *The Rainbow Chasers*. It is the story of a quest that lasted for nine long and frustrating years, and ended in triumph with a world's championship. It is a pursuit that was climaxed by a wild and joyous victory parade through the heart of the city that had watched, with varying degrees of ardor and disaffection, as a team was tormented by fate. Destiny, it seemed, was forever slipping the 76ers a whoopee cushion.

Nothing is quite so elusive, so ephemeral, as a rainbow's end. And each time it seemed as though the Sixers were about to arrive there, something happened. Usually, it was bad.

Their pursuit of the rainbow's end was best summed up one day by Chuck Daly, then an assistant coach with the 76ers. After a particularly frustrating loss in the playoffs, he sighed plaintively and said: "You know, this sure is a suffering business."

On the last day of May, 1983, savoring replaced suffering. That is when the 76ers won the National Basketball Association World Championship. That is when the City of Philadelphia blossomed with signs, signs that celebrated the arrival at rainbow's end, signs that alluded to the Sixers' center Moses Malone, signs that proclaimed:

The 11th Commandment:
THOU SHALT WIN IT ALL

The story of The Rainbow Chasers begins in August of 1974,

with the arrival in Philadelphia of Pat Williams, who had signed a three-year contract to become general manager of the 76ers. All of the negotiations between Pat and the Sixers' owner, Irv Kosloff, were conducted long distance. Pat was in Atlanta, Irv in Phoenix. Maybe that was symbolic; neither one of them, at the time they concluded their deal, was in Philadelphia. In those days, hardly anyone wanted to be identified with the 76ers. It was safer to say you were from out of town.

Only a few years before, the Sixers had been the best team in basketball. They had won the championship, had set what was then a regular season record for victories with a 68-13 mark. That was during 1966-67. What was expected to be a dynasty, however, never lasted past that one year. By the end of the decade, the team was sliding into despair and desperation. The Sixers' choices in the college drafts became so laughable that by the time the anti-Vietnam sentiment had peaked, when people howled "Abolish the draft," no one in Philadelphia was sure whether they meant the draft for the armed services or the Sixers.

In the period immediately preceding Pat's arrival, the team had even operated without a general manager. Clearly, then, no one was anxious to take the blame. There were so many dark clouds that you couldn't see the rainbow's end. But the chase began anyway.

And this is how it went . . .

1

Pass Me Another Brick

THEY CALLED HIM THE KANGAROO KID.

He had learned to play basketball in the asphalt jungle of Brooklyn, and there is no tougher proving ground. He was left-handed and he had a pasty, chalky complexion, but he was tougher than a strip of rawhide, and when he jumped it was like he had helium in his shorts.

Billy Cunningham was your typical gym rat, and there beat within him that pulsating rhythm of the game.

He had played on the last professional basketball team from Philadelphia to win the NBA championship. That was the 76ers of 1966–67, a team that would later be voted the best in the history of the league. It won 68 of its 81 regular season games, and then simply blew away the Cincinnati Royals, the Boston Celtics and the San Francisco Warriors in the playoffs. It was a monster team with all the components—quick, penetrating guards who could skewer you with their outside shooting (Hal Greer and Wali Jones); strong, powerful forwards who played "The Anvil Chorus" on the backboards (Chet Walker and Luke Jackson); and, at center, the most dominating player ever (Wilt Chamberlain).

The sixth man on that team, first one off the bench to inject enthusiasm whenever the team's pulse appeared to slacken, was The Kangaroo Kid.

They loved him in Philly.

But in 1969, Billy Cunningham jumped leagues, joining the American Basketball Association. No one was more heartbroken at Billy's departure than the owner of the Sixers at the time, Irv Kosloff. They had enjoyed a special relationship, Kos treating Billy with a benevolent, patronly sort of regard.

So here we were, in the summer of 1974, and the Sixers were still struggling to rise, Phoenix-like, from the ashes. After that 1966–67 title, they had slid slowly, but inexorably, from a once-proud, immensely successful franchise, to one that set records for incompetence that still stand. During the 1972–73 season, they had managed to play 82 games and win only nine. That is a standard of futility and frustration that remains without equal in the NBA; indeed, in just about any professional sport.

The following season, they had improved. Slightly. They had won 25 games, lost 57. Desperate now, they were locked in secret negotiations in an effort to bring back Billy Cunningham. There was a clause in Billy's contract specifying that if his ABA team, the Carolina Cougars, moved, he did not have to move with them and, if he chose, could bargain with other teams. Well, that spring, the Cougars' franchise had been switched to St. Louis, and Billy C. was not enthralled with that prospect.

When I arrived in Philadelphia to take over as the new general manager of the Sixers, Kos and a battery of lawyers were negotiating with Billy and his agent, Irwin Weiner. I arrived in Philly on a Sunday in August of '74, and the next morning we were off to New York to try to effect the return of the prodigal son to the Sixers.

First and foremost, this meant going one-on-one with Irwin Weiner. It wasn't the first time we had tangled. Irwin represented an All-Star forward on the Chicago Bulls, Bob Love, at the time I was the GM there in 1972. And when I was the GM in Atlanta, in 1973, one of our players, Herm Gilliam, also had retained Weiner.

We all knew we needed Billy C. back in Philly, for box office

18

reasons if no other. It was obvious he could not turn around a losing team all by himself. He was, by this time, in the twilight of his playing career. He was no longer the tireless, pugnacious Kangaroo Kid, but if his reflexes had slowed, his instincts had improved. He knew the game's intricacies and subtleties. He was still a great passer, he could still put down that jumpshot, he would still go barreling to the basket, and he never backed down. His competitive ferocity had not—still has not—diminished a bit. We knew he would give the team what it so badly needed at this point in time—a proven name, a recognizable attempt by the Sixers to regain respectability. He would be the first step on the road back.

We needed a foundation, and The Kangaroo Kid was the perfect cornerstone. He would be the first brick in what we hoped would be the construction of a new team.

Irwin Weiner, of course, knew all of this. And that didn't exactly help the Sixers' bargaining position.

A few words here about Irwin Weiner. Short. Kinky, curly red hair. A fondness for diamonds and long, thick cigars. The embodiment, in short, of the fast-talking, tough-talking, "Have-I-got-something-for-you-baby" agent. There is always a wreath of blue smoke around Irwin's head, and it definitely does not form a halo. He is the human version of the Sabra pear, which is native to Israel. It's tough and prickly on the outside but soft and appealing on the inside. That's Irwin. Gruff exterior, hard-nosed, but there is a warmth, a communicativeness on the inside. It just takes you a while to work your way through the rind.

Irwin had started in the garment district and later had dabbled in insurance. His benefactor was Walt Frazier, the All-Star guard for the New York Knicks. Walt introduced him to the NBA, and they became partners in the early 1970's, forming W-F Sports. Irwin's most famous client would end up being a Sixer just a couple of years later; a fellow by the name of Julius Erving.

Anyway, St. Louis, nee the Carolina Cougars, is not anxious to lose Billy Cunningham. Irwin Weiner does not exactly pull a gun on the Sixers, but he makes it clear The Kangaroo Kid will not come cheaply. We reach an agreement, finally, that is acceptable to

19

Weiner, Billy and the Sixers. He is signed to two years at $300,000 per year, with an option for a third year, at $400,000. Those were big, big numbers in those days.

And there was something else in that contract too.

It was a provision that, in the third year, Billy would collect one-half of his salary regardless of whether he was capable of playing *a single minute.*

Now this represented a considerable gamble on the part of the Sixers because Billy was regarded as what we in the trade call "damaged goods." He had undergone kidney surgery. Twice. No one is ever quite the same after going under the knife, of course, but it is always a more significant trauma for an athlete. The Sixers' coach, Gene Shue, frankly had some reservations about the wisdom of signing Billy. Not that he doubted Billy's talents or value, but he was worried about his health, how much those operations had sapped him. His concerns were certainly legitimate. Basketball is a game strictly for the healthy, after all.

So the papers were signed and Billy C. was now a Sixer once more.

Well, almost.

St. Louis would not relent. They refused to release him.

Talk about frustration. We had him, yet we didn't have him. What we had was the signature of Billy Cunningham on a contract, but not the player that went with the signature. The Sixers had opened training camp, but without The Kangaroo Kid. Billy, of course, was in limbo. He worked out on his own, practicing for a season he might never play. This stymie with St. Louis was ruining our promotional efforts, of course. Here we were with basically the same team that had managed in two years to win a total of 34 games while losing 130, and how could you expect anyone except the most masochistic to buy tickets? It was tough to sell this team to the public because there was nothing new.

Finally, in the fall, when camp was almost over and the season about to begin, St. Louis yielded. It was one of your basic Perry Mason kind of finishes, reached at almost the last possible moment. The settlement, in fact, was reached on the steps outside Federal Court in New York City. The Sixers paid St. Louis, which was strapped and stuggling, $125,000 in cash.

The Kangaroo Kid was back where he belonged.

And the sixers had made their first positive breakthrough after a long siege of torment and turmoil. They had a big-name player. He was in his thirties by now, and he had been twice operated on, but he still had some basketball left in him.

The first brick was in place.

There was another brick tantalizingly close at hand.

George McGinnis.

A blacksmith in sneakers. Arms like steel cables. A physique you could strike a match on. He had played for Indiana University and he was so strong, so skilled, that it was quickly obvious he belonged in the pros. The Sixers had drafted him in 1973 on the second round. But George wanted no part of Philadelphia. Or, for that matter, the NBA. Two years earlier he had signed with the ABA, with the Indiana entry, so he could remain in his native state.

As a pro, he was all that had been expected. He had led his team to ABA championships twice, and all the Sixers could do was look on forlornly and try to disguise their lustful drooling.

McGinnis' agent was none other than Irwin Weiner.

We talked to Weiner, asked him to relay to George our burning desire to acquire him. But George reiterated his previous position. He liked playing in Indiana. He had no interest in Philly. Privately, you had to think, who could blame him? He was winning championships in Indiana while the Sixers were counting winning streaks on one finger.

But there was another NBA team that coveted McGinnis almost as much as the Sixers, and that was the New York Knicks. So we talked to Mike Burke, who was then president of the Knicks, and to Red Holzman, their general manager and coach. It had become painfully obvious to us that to continue sitting around and brooding about George wasn't accomplishing anything other than making our ulcers fester. Why pine for someone when the object of your afffections is patently not interested? We finally came to the realization that if George McGinnis was never going to end up as a 76er, and all we ever got out of it was his draft rights, what good was any of that? But maybe he would be interested in playing for another team in the NBA.

Like New York.

So we arrived at one of those midnight deals with the Knicks. If *they* could sign George, if they could lure him away from Indiana, then we would surrender our draft rights to them. In return, we would receive Earl Monroe, a first round pick, and six figures' worth of cash. That wasn't bad. It wasn't George, but then Earl the Pearl was a spectacular showman at guard and, being a native Philadelphian, he would bring out a lot of people. Plus, a first round pick might give us another brick for our building job. The cash was incidental, but, hey, you never turn down green stuff.

We insisted on one important provision in our agreement with the Knicks: The only way the deal would work is they had to sign McGinnis by early October, 1974; specifically, by one week prior to the start of the regular season.

Well, early October came, and so did the deadline we had agreed on. And so did a phone call from Mike Burke.

"George has turned us down," he said, with considerable regret.

There, it appeared, went another brick. The deadline had come and gone and George McGinnis was not a Knick, and he sure wasn't a 76er, either. So our deal with New York was negated. We didn't get Earl Monroe or the draft pick or the cash. Or George McGinnis.

Mostly what we got was another heavy dose of frustration.

Bricks sure are hard to come by.

So the Sixers began the 1974–75 season. Not exactly hopeful. But hoping.

The roster wasn't exactly a rollcall of Hall of Famers. It included players like LeRoy Ellis, Harvey Catchings, Allan Bristow, Tom VanArsdale, Fred Boyd, Fred Carter and Steve Mix. Steve would make the All-Star team that year. And Billy Cunningham was, at long last, a Sixer, and making solid contributions. During this season, we would trade VanArsdale for Clyde Lee from Atlanta, trying to strengthen our rebounding. We needed a force inside, but the force we wanted was still back home in Indiana. Gene Shue did a commendable job of coaching and the 76ers weren't all that bad, increasing their win total from the previous season by nine, up to 34, and they were in the hunt for a playoff spot until the final month.

The major bright spot of that season was the emergence of Doug Collins, who was in his second year but, in all actuality, was a rookie. He had been forced to miss most of the first year because he had broken a bone in his foot, the severest sort of fracture, so bad, in fact, that surgeons had to transplant a piece of his hipbone to his foot. He had spent his first months as a professional in a cast and on crutches, and the critics had a field day. The Sixers got stuck with another horrendous No. 1 draft choice, they said. The 76ers either draft players who can't play, or they wind up with the lame, the halt and the blind.

This season, .however, their criticism was muffled. Doug Collins, finally healthy, began to fulfill the potential everyone realized he had.

I had first heard of Doug Collins while I was the GM with the Chicago Bulls. In the winter of 1971–72 the sports pages of the Chicago papers were ablaze with his name. Almost every day, it seemed, you'd open the paper to this headline: REDBIRDS WIN; 42 FOR COLLINS. So who, exactly, was Doug Collins?

The answer was a skinny, furiously competitive, sweet-shooting, 6–6 kid who played guard for Illinois State. On February 23, 1972, the Bulls' coach, Dick Motta, and I travel to DeKalb, Illinois, to see Illinois State play at Northern Illinois University. We see a classic. Doug Collins scores 33 points, including the winning basket, and Illinois State wins 86–85. For a long time on the drive back to Chicago, neither of us says anything. Maybe we were afraid to; maybe we couldn't believe what we had seen. But I had a tingle in my gut. I felt like the baseball scout must have felt when he first saw Mickey Mantle as a fifteen-year-old. Here was this basketball player who was big, quick, rangy, so enthusiastic, so competitive, with all the obvious bloodlines of a winner.

Finally, Dick looked at me and said: "I want him."

It was like his words hung there in the winter darkness.

That was Doug's junior year. It was also around the time the NBA hardship draft rule came along, which meant a college player could claim financial deprivation and turn professional before completing his college eligibility. Both Dick and I were convinced that Doug Collins wouldn't require another year of college seasoning; he was ready now.

I called an attorney in Chicago I had known for some time, Herb Rudoy, and asked him if he would act as sort of an emissary for us, go down to the Illinois State campus and talk to this Doug Collins and tell him the Chicago Bulls were interested in him, and did he share their interest? Herb made the trip. The kid, he reported, was flattered. Also flabbergasted.

But not interested.

For two reasons, neither of which, in all honesty, we could argue with. First, Doug didn't want his family carrying that "hardship" stigma. He grew up in Benton, a small town in southern Illinois in an area known as "Little Egypt." He grew up with a hoop in his driveway, a freshly scrubbed sort of kid who had been weaned on honesty. And, second, which was in keeping with Doug's personality and his own sense of patriotism, he had been invited to try out for a spot on the 1972 Olympic team. He made that team, of course, ended up rooming with Bobby Jones, and they played probably the most memorable international basketball game ever, against the Russians, in the Munich Olympics. Doug would go on to have a great senior year at Illinois State and become a unanimous first-team All-American. By the time he became eligible for the draft, in 1973, he was hardly a secret. It was at this stage that the Sixers were coming off that disastrous 9-73 season, the only benefit of which was that they got to pick first. They were enamored of our center in Chicago, big Clifford Ray, so we offered them Ray, plus veteran guard Bob Weiss, in exchange for their first

24

choice in the draft. We would make that, of course, Collins.

The problem was that Ray had a bad knee, and our deal with the Sixers hinged on Cliff passing a physical. The Bulls' team physician said he was fine. But Ray's agent, a Philadelphia attorney named Richie Phillips, takes Clifford to two physicians, one of them being Phillips' brother, and they say Ray's knee needs surgery. Mind you, all of this is now happening only the night before the draft. Kevin Loughery has resigned as coach of the Sixers in the meantime and Jack McMahon, the director of personnel, quickly moves into a position of influence. Jack is a shrewd judge of talent. He says, "Forget the deal with Chicago completely. Philadelphia doesn't want Clifford Ray and Bobby Weiss, Philadelphia wants Doug Collins." So the deal is dead and the Sixers draft Doug Collins, and all he does is go on to make the All-Star team five times. The good part for me is that two years later I will end up in Philly just as Doug is realizing his potential.

By the winter of the 1974–75 season, it has become obvious that what the rebuilding Sixers need is a center. The most dominant big man in the college ranks at that time is Marvin Webster, a senior at Morgan State. The Human Eraser. Doesn't just block shots, he inhales them. The two best big juniors in the collegiate ranks are Robert Parish and Leon Douglas, and the only other young 7-footer on the horizon is sophomore Tree Rollins. The Sixers' prospects for immediate help in the middle didn't look very promising. Sometimes, when you're really desperate, you'll try anything. Which is what the Sixers did next.

The previous fall, a young player named Moses Malone, from Petersburg, Virginia, had finished his senior year in high school and had signed to enroll at the University of Maryland. But he never attended a class there. He went, instead, directly into the pros, signing with Utah, an ABA franchise. All he did was average 18.8 points a game, play 3,200 minutes, grab 1,200 rebounds and shoot 57 percent from the floor. All as a nineteen-year-old who should have been a freshman in college.

Malone's stunning debut, even though it was in what was dismissed as "that other league," led to speculation: Was there another high-school phenom out there ready for the pros? It so happened that *The New York Times* ran an article in December of '74, reporting that the three best prospects among the high-school seniors were 6–8 Bill Willoughby of Englewood, New Jersey, 6–11 Bill Cartwright of Elk Grove, California, and 6–10 Darryl Dawkins of Orlando, Florida. What did the Sixers have to lose? We were willing to rob the cradle if that's what it took. So I sent Jocko Collins, a baseball and basketball scout, to check on Willoughby, and Jack McMahon, Jr., to look at Cartwright. In the meantime, I phoned an old friend from my baseball days, pitcher Jim Kaat, who may still be on a mound somewhere when he's 109. Kaat lived in Apopka, Florida, at the time, and I asked him to check out this big high-school center at Maynard Evans High in Orlando. He phoned back and said: "You better see this kid for yourself." So Jocko went down, and came back and said: "This kid's only eighteen, but he's built like Luke Jackson. He's a brute already." So now we sent Jack McMahon down, and it was an instant love affair.

Jack says: "We've got to get him. He's already a man physically."

This was getting scary.

So I went down to Florida in early March and I could see why everyone was so worked up. Darryl was immense, and his head was shaven at the time, which added to his menacing aura. He was a man playing a game with boys.

There was still one person whose blessing was needed—Gene Shue, the coach of the Sixers. If he had been turned off by Darryl, we never would have pursued him. So Gene, during an off day, went to Jacksonville, where Darryl's team was playing in the state high-school tournament finals. I couldn't wait for Gene to get back to Philly to find out his reaction. I was in Greensboro, North Carolina, scouting talent, and from a pay phone, at midnight, I called him at his motel in Jacksonville. Now Gene is usually a very deliberate person. But this time he never hesitated. "Let's go with him," is all he said.

The next person who had to be sold was Irv Kosloff. Kos is basically conservative, and the revolutionary idea of going after a kid who was still in high school must have really seemed idiotic to him at the time, but he could sense our excitement, so he said to go ahead.

I called Herb Rudoy, the Chicago attorney, and said: "Remember three years ago when I asked you to find out if Doug Collins was interested in playing pro basketball for Chicago? Well, this time I want you to go to Orlando and see what kind of interest a fellow named Darryl Dawkins has in the Philadelphia 76ers. Incidentally, you should know this fellow is a senior in high school." There was a long silence. Herb may have been trying to smother his laughter. Herb makes the trip, probably doubting our sanity all the way, and calls back to say Darryl Dawkins will be pleased and proud to play for the 76ers—for a $100,000 bonus for signing and for $200,000 a year for seven years. Clearly, it was not just Darryl's physique that was big. His imagination knew no bounds, either.

Herb talks to Darryl's mother and sells her on the idea. So now it looks like the Sixers have captured a closely guarded secret. And a very promising brick. The trick now is to *keep* Darryl Dawkins a secret. We have to make him invisible, and when you're in the neighborhood of 6–10 and 250 pounds, that's not exactly easy. We can't allow him to play in any of the usual post-season all-star tournaments they have for high-school blue chippers because we don't want any of the NBA teams that are drafting ahead of us to know about him. So we successfully baby-sit Darryl, doing everything short of locking him in a closet.

The Sixers had the fifth pick in the first round of the 1975 draft. The draft went according to plan. David Thompson was selected first, followed by David Meyers, Marvin Webster and Alvan Adams. The No. 5 pick, by Philadelphia, is Darryl Dawkins. Everyone wonders what college he played for, and when they find out that, uh, well, he just got out of high school, you could hear the snickers from the other NBA teams.

Before the draft Herb and I had flown to Orlando to conclude the deal and officially sign Darryl. We meet in the law offices of Paul Perkins. With Attorney Perkins is the Reverend Mr. William Judge, the Dawkins' minister. We take a lunch break, and Lawyer Perkins departs with Darryl's mother. Upon their return, they pull the pin from the hand grenade and announce that the Reverend Mr. Judge will act as Darryl Dawkins' financial adviser. Herb Rudoy, who has done all the work, sees that he is about to be niftily cut out of the deal. Goodbye to a hefty agent's percentage. And now it looks like goodbye Darryl for the Sixers. The deal, so close to consummation, is about to collapse. Another brick is floating out the door. We finally, frantically, convince Herb to accept a smaller percentage. This mollifies Herb only slightly. He turns to the Reverend Mr. Judge and says: "This isn't right. You're a man of the cloth." And the Reverend Mr. Judge turns to Herb and replies: "Mr. Rudoy, there are many kinds of reverends, and *I* is a financial reverend."

Herb is apoplectic, of course. He's ready to walk out. I whack him in the ribs and whisper: "You wouldn't even be here if it wasn't for us bringing you in. For heaven's sake, go along with the program. A smaller percentage is better than no percentage at all."

Incredibly, one other obstacle remains before we finally acquire Darryl. That is his high-school coach, Fred Pennington. He had been very helpful to the Sixers. We'd used him to keep Darryl out of those all-star games and to fend off about 200 colleges that wanted to recruit Darryl, plus some pro bird dogs, and without his cooperation we might never have landed Darryl. Now Fred gets wind of the deal between the reverend and the lawyer and he thinks there should be something in it for him. So we make him the official Florida scout for the Philadelphia 76ers, at $5,000 a year for seven years. That wasn't bad for glorified baby-sitting.

The final cost of acquiring a high-school senior was $1.4 million over seven seasons, *plus* a hundred grand to get his signature, *plus* another 35 thou to appease his coach. And what we did, of course, had never been done before in the history of the NBA—draft a kid right from high school into the pros. But the Sixers' position at the time was one of: What might he develop into?

Was he going to grow five more inches? Would we end up with a center who was 7–3 and 290 pounds? The prospects were intriguing. He certainly didn't lack for self-confidence. And in that regard, I got a preview of just what sort of flamboyance we had acquired when Darryl moved to Philadelphia to play in the summer Baker League. I phoned his apartment and was greeted, not by some shy, anxiety-ridden high-school kid, but by this booming bass voice which cheerfully said: "Hello, this is the Dawk, and I'm ready to talk." I was too taken aback to have the presence of mind to snap back: "Hello, this is Pat and I'm ready to chat."

All we knew at this point was that we were reasonably sure we had landed not just a brick but a potential boulder for the 76ers.

Before going into that 1975 draft, we had decided that if one young giant was good, two would be even better. We were willing to take a *second* high-school senior—Bill Willoughby. If he was still there when it was our turn to pick fifth in the second round, we'd take him, and probably succeed in reducing every other NBA team to helpless guffaws. ("Hey, look, the Sixers are taking another high-school kid! Who you gonna draft in the third round, a kindergartner?") Except Atlanta, which picked just before Philly in the second round, smelled a rat. Word had gotten around that we had already signed Willoughby before the draft, which we had, and the Atlanta folks decided this kid wouldn't be listed among the draftees if *someone* didn't want him, and for a very good reason. So Atlanta drafted Willoughby—without ever having seen him play!

So now we have our second-round pick, but Willoughby is no longer available, plucked right out from under us. We picked, instead, a guard whom Jack McMahon liked very much. His name was Lloyd Free, and he was from little Guilford College, in Guilford, North Carolina. His freshman year his team had won the NAIA championship.

Lloyd's coach was Jack Jensen, and he and I had gone to Wake Forest together. Jack kept calling me, saying: "I don't want to lose

Lloyd, but his time has come. He's good enough for the NBA right now."

After their regular season, some of the Guilford team entered an AAU tournament in Baton Rouge, one of those little-known tournaments that hardly anyone hears about, where the players outnumber the crowd. But Jack McMahon, that marvelous talent scout, who knows more backroads than Atlas, was there. He was the only pro scout in attendance. Lloyd Free went to the free throw line 27 times in one game, demonstrating his exceptional driving ability, his fearlessness, his ability to take over a game offensively. Lloyd was represented by Joseph Jeffries-El, who had been his benefactor since all the way back in high school, sensing that someday Lloyd Free would be worth a lot of money. When we drafted Lloyd, Joe-El, as he liked to be called, said simply: "Philadelphia just got itself a miniature Oscar Robertson."

Here we were searching around for bricks and this agent was confidently telling us we'd just landed a brick right out of Fort Knox.

We paved the way for another brick in the winter of 1975. His name was Caldwell Jones.

When I was the general manager in Chicago, we had acquired Dennis Awtrey, a center, from Philadelphia. In return, we had given the Sixers our second-round pick in the 1973 draft. They had used it to take Caldwell Jones out of Albany State, in Georgia. He was a lean, angular 7-footer, shaped like a stiletto, and my reaction at the time was, boy, the Sixers bungled that pick. This guy doesn't have enough heft. He'll never last in the NBA: he doesn't have enough meat and he'll get pushed all over the place. But Jack Mc-Mahon had watched him play, and every time the other team took a shot, Caldwell Jones was stamping it: Return To Sender. As usual, Jack's instincts were right on target. But the Sixers had failed to sign Caldwell because he wanted a guaranteed contract and they weren't willing to give him one.

CJ played in the summer league, the Baker League, in Philly that year, and was devastating, chewing up everyone. Word of what he was doing traveled three thousand miles out to California, where Wilt Chamberlain was coaching the San Diego Conquistadors of the ABA. San Diego signed Caldwell and got a steal. They were willing to give him a no-cut contract for three years, at only $60,000 a year. Caldwell promptly becomes a starter at center for San Diego, and in the 1973–74 season averages 15 points a game and gets almost 1,100 rebounds. All of which is a source of considerable embarrassment to the Sixers, who have no quality center of their own, and the one they could have had is taken right from under their noses. Caldwell's second year is even better. He is an offensive force, averaging almost 20 points a game, collecting over 1,000 rebounds. But the ABA is in turmoil, with franchises collapsing everywhere.

So on February 25, 1975, the Sixers sign Caldwell Jones for future delivery. His contract is to take effect with Philadelphia in the fall of 1976, at the conclusion of his three-year contract with San Diego.

This turns out to be a significant move on the Sixers' part because when what is left of the ABA is merged with the NBA, the players are all thrown into a common pool and dispersed through a draft. If the Sixers hadn't secured Caldwell's draft rights initially, and then signed that for-future-delivery contract with him, he probably would have ended up someplace else.

It is difficult to remember, but while all of this frenetic wheeling and dealing involving Dawkins and Free and McGinnis and Jones has been going on, the Sixers are playing basketball. They miss the playoffs in the spring of 1975, but in the meantime a lot of bricks have been collected for the rebuilding during the summer.

And the biggest brick of all is about to fall into place . . . .

On Easter weekend of 1975, George McGinnis' contract with Indiana had expired. On May 30, a story breaks in the papers that the New York Knicks have signed him.

Talk about trauma in the Sixers' office!

Here the Sixers owned the draft rights to George, had

31

passionately pursued him for years, and the Knicks just plunged right in and signed him. So the Sixers reacted just the way you'd expect someone who feels he is wronged to react in this age of litigation. The Sixers hired an attorney.

Not just any attorney.

Louis B. Nizer.

The Wilt Chamberlain of attorneys.

In June, at the NBA owners meeting in San Francisco, the first meeting presided over by Lawrence O'Brien as the league's new commissioner, Nizer made an impassioned plea in behalf of the Sixers. It was pure William Jennings Bryan "ye-shall-not-crucify-man-on-a-cross-of-gold" type oratory. He attacked the Knicks for their arrogance, their blatant high-handedness, their callous and impudent disregard for the rules, their bald effrontery at signing another team's player.

The owners were moved to give Nizer a standing ovation.

And the Commissioner came down hard on the Knicks. O'Brien revoked New York's signing of George McGinnis. But he didn't stop there. Not only could the Knicks not have McGinnis, but they were also fined and stripped of their first-round draft pick for the following year.

The Sixers felt vindicated.

But there was still a problem, because in signing George, the Knicks had set a price on him, and it was staggering—$500,000 just for signing to play in the NBA, and a salary of $400,000 a year for five years.

Now it began to look as if the Sixers had gained a pyrrhic victory. New York's deal with George had been revoked by the Commissioner, and he had ruled that if McGinnis belonged to anybody, it was to the Sixers. But all the 76ers heard from George and his agent, Irwin Weiner, was silence. Philadelphia still, apparently, held no allure at all for George.

Then, on July 10, 1975, I called Weiner at his New York offices, just trying to keep some sort of dialogue going. We had had the door slammed in our faces all along, but we kept trying to wedge a toe in there.

32

"Irwin," I said over the phone, "why don't we just sign George tonight and get all of this nonsense resolved?"

I was throwing out a fishing line, with no real hope of getting a bite. And Irwin, with a strange sense of urgency in his voice, replied: "Yes, let's do it. Get up here immediately!"

The phone line hadn't gone dead and I was already halfway to the 30th Street Station to grab a train for New York. Sid Bluming, a sharp young lawyer with Nizer's firm, met me in the NBA office and we hammered out an all-nighter. Kos wanted some sort of relief from the Knicks, feeling that the Sixers deserved something. He was also convinced we should sign George now and seek relief later. This was too close to consummation to bother with petty revenge now.

Shortly after midnight, George McGinnis was signed as a 76er.

That would be the turning point for professional basketball in Philadelphia. The Sixers had the brick they had pursued for so long.

And Commissioner O'Brien had a sort of triumph for himself, luring one of the biggest names from the other league to the NBA, and then placing him with the team that was the weak sister at the time.

So now, in the summer of 1975, this woeful, struggling, floundering team had George McGinnis, Darryl Dawkins, Lloyd Free, and Caldwell Jones on the horizon. For the first time in years, there was an air of expectancy as it came time for training camp.

And then, on Labor Day, another altogether unexpected brick fell from the sky. Richie Phillips, an aggressive, flamboyant Philadelphia lawyer, called me and asked: "If a drafted player has not been tendered a contract by September, is he then a free agent?"

"That," I told him, "is my understanding."

"Well," he said, "I represent Joe Bryant. He was drafted 14th overall, by Golden State, but they still haven't sent him a contract. If he's a free agent, would you be interested in signing him?"

Suddenly it's raining bricks on the Sixers. For years they've been scraping and scuffling for some semblance of talent, and now they're being handed one, gift wrapped. Joe Bryant is 6–10 and can play all five positions. Plus, having graduated from Bartram High and LaSalle College in Philly, he's a natural local draw. Golden State, which had made Bryant its first choice, had simply made a clerical error. They had forgotten to put a blank contract in the mail to Bryant.

So on September 12, 1975, JB became a Sixer, at $140,000 a year for five years. (Jelly Bean has played eight seasons in the NBA since.)

Now, as camp approaches, the team has a whole new look, and for the first time in a long time there is an interest in pro basketball in Philly.

Funny thing about bricks. Sometimes you can't find one, and then one day they back a truck up to your door and dump out enough to build a wall.

2

Let George Do It

GEORGE MCGINNIS HAD MUSCLES in places where most people don't even have places.

We're talking Stud City.

Football coaches took one look at that sculpted physique and they swooned. He was big and strong and sleek and fast and probably would have made a run at a gold medal in the decathlon in the Olympics, which is generally regarded as the yardstick by which the "world's greatest athlete" is measured.

George was one of those people for whom everything, but especially basketball, came easily. Maybe too easily. And, in the end, that blessing might have been his curse.

He was a natural. Sadly, that would turn out to be his fatal flaw. Because he had these stunning gifts he never really had to work, and as a result lapsed into some bad work habits.

Anyway, the 76ers began training camp for the 1975–76 season at Ursinus College, in Collegeville, Pennsylvania, and those were exciting times. It would end up being probably the most chronicled training camp in NBA history.

The Sixers, after all, had an 18-year-old fresh from high school

(Darryl Dawkins) and this hot-shot guard from a tiny college (Lloyd Free) and a local playground legend (Joe Bryant) and a hero from the past glory years (Billy Cunningham) on their roster.

But most of all, they had George McGinnis. Along with Julius Erving, McGinnis was the biggest name in the ABA, and the curious were beside themselves wondering if he could have as much of an impact on the older, more established league.

The Sixers launched a saturation advertising campaign. They plastered the city with billboards, all of them with this huge portrait of George McGinnis in a Sixers uniform. Emblazoned across all the advertisements was a recurrent theme, worded in two different slogans. One—"Let George Do It"—suggested that upon the brawny back of George McGinnis the Sixers would be borne to the top. The other slogan—"By George, We've Got It"—was a hardly subtle promise that the 76ers, the team you have been snickering at these last few seasons, have gone out and got themselves a whole herd of prime beef, and this guy here, McGinnis, is the boss bull.

Training camp went well. For the most part. There was all this oozing of talent and great expectations, and the Sixers, indeed, looked like contenders.

There was, however, one disquieting aspect.

And it involved George McGinnis.

He was a corner-cutter.

In every practice drill, in every lap run, George always did the minimum, just enough to get by. It wasn't that he was challenging the coach or the system, or that he was staging some sort of private rebellion. George was just doing what came naturally. To him. He took the easy way out. It would prove, later, to be his undoing, as well as a source of many of the frustrations the Sixers would experience.

No one said anything about it. No one wrote about it. Maybe none of us wanted to think about it. Maybe the media assumed that George McGinnis was one of those athletes who are notoriously poor practice players and can't seem to get turned on until the game starts. Such players have been legion in all sports, after all. And George wasn't being paid to look like a million (or, in his case, $2.5

36

million) when it didn't really count.

That, at least, was how his less-than-inspired practices were rationalized away at the time. What no one had the foresight to consider, however, was that the younger players would tend to follow whatever example the star set. Players are great imitators. If George was careless and disinterested during practice, they assumed they could get by behaving the same way. The difference, though, was that George already had become as good as he was going to be, and the others had not. In the end, they only cheated themselves.

So the 1975–76 season began. On the road. The 76ers' opener was at Chicago. It was a victory. The home opener was, through a scheduling aberration, on a Monday night, which meant bucking some tough competition from NFL football on TV. But the opponent was Los Angeles, always a big draw, and there was the added excitement of the home debut of Big George.

The Spectrum was stuffed. And the Sixers creamed the Lakers and George was magnificent, scoring, rebounding, controlling the game in virtually every area. He was an instant hit with the people of Philly, who are not always so easily won over.

But they took to George immediately. He had sizzle and crackle, and home attendance immediately increased from an average of 7,237 per game the year before to 12,432. And every one of those five thousand extra spectators came because of George.

His impact cannot be overstated. The day he set a sneakered foot in Philadelphia was the day pro basketball arrived in this city as a big-time sport.

Thus, the season was launched on a high note. There were several sell-outs. George was all he had been advertised. And Doug Collins was coming into his prime. Lloyd Free was busting out with some big scoring nights, his rawness painfully evident on some occasions but his potential undeniable. It was a nice blend, a promising one: of youngsters, the established star in George, and the reliable veterans, especially Steve Mix and Billy Cunningham.

And then, when it looked as if things couldn't be better, they got worse.

Billy Cunningham went down.

He would never get back up.

A Friday night in December in the Spectrum. The Sixers against the Knicks. A big crowd. New York usually draws well anyway, but this time the rivalry was extra special because, remember, it was those dastardly Knicks, those smug New Yorkers, who had tried to steal George McGinnis away from Philly.

Billy C, who was still outstanding in an open court, had the ball and was driving. He had just put the ball on the floor around the free throw line and was about to make his move, a cross-over dribble. Butch Beard was defending against him. Billy tried to evade him.

There was no contact.

But as he tried to push off and accelerate in a new direction, Billy's knee buckled. Everything in the knee was shredded. You could literally hear that knee coming apart.

And right after that you heard this shriek, this awful, frightening scream of pain, a howling of agony so terrible that even the people in the upper deck winced and clapped their hands to their ears.

Billy crumpled in a heap, clutching at his knee.

There would be a picture of him in the next morning's *Inquirer*, lying there, writhing, grabbing at that knee, his mouth open. It was the sort of picture you look at and you are stabbed by the pain he must have felt. That photograph would win a lot of prizes later on. It's one you see at 3 in the morning when you awake with the screaming sweats from some terrible nightmare.

Where Billy went down was, ironically, almost the same spot where Luke Jackson had also collapsed, almost to the same day, in 1968. Luke's Achilles' tendon had snapped, and that injury had basically ended his career. Now, seven years later, in the same building, Billy C had come to the same tragic end.

I remember talking to Dr. Joseph Torg, who was the Sixers' team physician at the time, and he said: "Everything that could be damaged in Billy's knee has been damaged."

The Kangaroo Kid was through as a player.

Oh, he would try to come back. Oh, how he would try. Through surgery, through rehabilitation, but even his marvelous determination wasn't enough. He tried to return to training camp the next year but it became obvious soon enough that his knee, for all of the surgeons' snipping and tucking and for all of his weight work, was never going to be the same.

When they carried him off the Spectrum floor that night, it was like a black cloud dropped over the squad. To a degree, he had been the heart of the team. I remember going to a pancake house for breakfast the next morning and looking at the newspaper rack, and there on the front page was that picture of Billy holding his knee, and the tears just rushed down my cheeks uncontrollably. It was a powerful picture, but the implications of it were even more overpowering.

Here were the Sixers, coming back from oblivion, a team with that special look, and now this . . . .

Worse was to see a fine athlete and a genuinely nice person cut down so abruptly. Little did anyone know at the time that two seasons later Billy C would be back with the Sixers in a totally different capacity.

The winter of 1975–76 wound on and the team became not only respectable, but a consistent winner. The Sixers won 46 games, lost 36. For the first time in five seasons, they made the playoffs. They ended up tied with Buffalo for second place in the Atlantic Division, 10 games over .500, and within hailing distance of Boston. The promised turnaround had materialized. And George McGinnis had lived up to every adjective-splattered anthem of praise. He had averaged 23 points a game and 12.6 rebounds, sixth in the league in both categories. He had made the All-Star team. He had proven impressively that he could dominate in the NBA as easily as he had in the suspect ABA.

It must be mentioned that during the season, George McGinnis had shouldered a crushing burden. But he had responded admirably. He had never balked at those advertising campaigns that put the pressure squarely on him. He had just shrugged and said, "Fine," and gone out and played. Now came the playoffs and there was tremendous anticipation because it had been in the playoffs in the ABA where George had been so awesome. He had consistently carried his Indiana team to great heights, all the way to two titles, and there was every reason to believe he would do the same in Philadelphia.

Realistically, you couldn't expect an NBA championship right away, not with a team still building. But the first round of the playoffs, a best-of-3 miniseries with Buffalo, seemed a cinch. The Sixers had the home court advantage, for starters.

Which they promptly blew.

The first game of the playoffs fell on a Thursday night in the Spectrum. The 15th of April. Income tax day.

The Sixers do not play well. George McGinnis struggles. Buffalo wins, 95-89

After all of this regular season success, after using all of these bricks to build what appears to be a solid foundation, the team makes its first appearance on center stage in half a decade and promptly performs an inglorious pratfall. Worse, the Sixers must now play the very next night, in Buffalo, on Good Friday, and the possibility of being eliminated in two straight suddenly seems very real.

Wrong again.

Buffalo has Bob McAdoo, who led the NBA in scoring three straight years; plus Randy Smith, a fine all-around player, and Ernie DiGregorio, as its leaders. But the Sixers play an aroused game and George McGinnis is brilliant. It's a Philadelphia avalanche—Sixers 131, Buffalo 106.

And in this game Buffalo suffers not only a thrashing but the loss of one of their principal rebounders, John Shumate. In one of those mid-air tangles around the backboard, Shumate is flipped and lands on his head with a horrible, sickening sound. He is carried off on a stretcher, unconscious, and the report from the hospital is that he has a concussion.

He was fortunate he was not killed, his skull shattered.

Now the playoff is even, a game apiece, and the good omens all seem to have swung back to the Sixers. The final game will be played on April 18, Easter Sunday, back in the Spectrum.

It will mark the first of what will be a long line of crowd disappointments in Philly. Only 13,000 fans show up for the game. True, it is unseasonably hot, the temperature outside in the high eighties, and they have had short notice, hardly anyone expecting a third game would be required after the Sixers' poor performance 72 hours earlier. Still, it was expected there would be a full house, not to mention thousands of turnaways.

But there wasn't. Maybe they sensed what was to come and had no stomach for it.

It was a gut-buster of a game.

In one sequence, Harvey Catchings of the Sixers blocked *five* consecutive Buffalo shots. And, with the game tied and only two seconds left to play, Freddie Carter had rattled in a jumpshot to put the Sixers ahead by two. The 76ers, it seemed almost certain, would survive.

But it was all a tease.

McAdoo puts up the shot that will tie the game but misses. He follows it. To everyone in the building it seems McAdoo fouls Clyde Lee of the Sixers going for that rebound. To everyone in the building it seems that way except to the person who matters the most at that moment. One of the referees, Jake O'Donnell, at the final buzzer, whistles Clyde Lee for the foul.

Time has expired. The game is over. The Sixers are ahead by two.

But McAdoo gets to go to the free throw line. If he makes *both*, there is overtime. One miss, and the Sixers win.

The Spectrum is an absolute asylum.

One of the Sixers' fans, unable to contain himself, wraps his arms around the basket support and begins to shake it violently. The basket sways wildly. McAdoo will have to shoot at a moving target.

41

The security guards peel the fan off the basket support. And in the midst of this crucible, Bob McAdoo shoots his free throws.

He makes them.

It cuts the heart right out of the Sixers. They hang in there and fight gallantly, but they lose. In overtime: Buffalo 124, Philadelphia 123.

And the Sixers lose with George McGinnis out of the game. He had fouled out while the game is still in regulation and still being hotly contested. His sixth personal is a silly reach-in, a serve-no-purpose, totally unnecessary kind of foul. And it has come at the very height of the war. It seems a blatant effort by George to bail out, as though he had had enough and he wanted out of the game.

That is the harshest sort of judgment to make, of course.

And there was a reluctance to want to believe that had been the case. Here was the player who had been the Sixers' savior all season and now, at the moment of truth, he had backed off? That was too crushing to contemplate. So some people took their solace from remembering George's track record, his past performances of always delivering under pressure in the ABA, and they decided—or, hoped—that this was simply an aberration.

Too, he had become so popular with the fans, and he had a knack for manipulating the media, of never hiding, of saying what seemed precisely appropriate, and with such sincerity, that it was written off as a poor performance, but uncharacteristic. After all, George McGinnis had done so much for basketball in Philadelphia, it seemed almost heresy to crucify him now. It was easier just to assume this would never happen again.

But it would, of course.

And what we had seen was a harbinger of things to come, an ominous foreshadowing of frustration that would haunt the Sixers in the playoffs for what would seem almost forever, and which would eventually end in George's exile.

But of all the playoff failures, this one would be remembered as the cruelest. Its pain would linger the longest. Its memories would make mocking sounds for years.

42

I still remember, in fact, walking down Broad Street a week later. It was a hot spring day and the wind was whipping, people hunched against it as they walked. You had to keep blinking your eyes to keep out the soot and the grime that collects in a large city's streets over the winter. And as I walked, head down, part of a week-old newspaper swirled past me and, for a moment, lodged against the curbing and flipped open. It flipped open to the sports page from the day following that playoff loss to Buffalo. The first thing my eyes fell on, instinctively, was a picture of Bob McAdoo and Clyde Lee going up for that rebound, and the resulting foul call that forced the overtime.

The game that the Sixers had won . . . and yet hadn't.

It was like it wouldn't go away.

So the 1975–76 season had ended sourly, as stale and tattered as that week-old newspaper that lay tauntingly on the sidewalk.

Still, you could sift through the ashes of that playoff loss and find some hopeful embers.

Basketball had returned to a place of prominence in Philadelphia. George McGinnis' first year had been, on balance, a smash . . . provided you didn't think too hard, linger too long, over the playoffs. And the young players had looked promising. Doug Collins was playing like perpetual motion. Lloyd Free could come in and light up the joint with his rainbow jumpshots. Darryl Dawkins had been spoon-fed his first year, nursed along, and everyone was convinced the gamble would be justified.

There was, in short, a lot to look forward to. The future seemed to burgeon with promise. And after several years of confusion and struggling, the Sixers at last were a winning team. Most important, for once things looked solid. There wouldn't be this continuing revolving door of change. Life had settled down.

For about, oh, 30 seconds . . . .

The phone rings and it is Nat Budin. He is Irv Kosloff's attorney. What would the owner's lawyer want to talk about in May?

"I would like for you to come, *immediately*, to the nineteenth floor of the United Engineers Building," he said.

"Oh, yes, bring Gene Shue and Jack McMahon with you."

The coach, it turned out, was in Cherry Hill, New Jersey, that very moment. In the dentist's chair. But Jack was with me.

"Sure, Nat," I said. "What's up?"

Something in his voice made me feel as if I had just swallowed an ice cube. Whole.

"You'll find out," he said, "when you get here."

So Jack and I hurried over to the United Engineers Building, up to the nineteenth floor, and we were ushered into a conference room. Kos is there, and his first words hiss through the air like shrapnel . . . .

3

Meet Your New Owner

THE CONFERENCE ROOM was one of those opulent places that makes you feel you should genuflect before entering. Dark wooden paneling, polished to a deep luster. Thick carpeting, ankle-deep. Ornate furnishings. The whole atmosphere bespoke wealth and power. You had the feeling that destinies, lives, fortunes, all were determined in a room like this, and no one spoke above a whisper.

Waiting almost inside the door was Irv Kosloff, the owner of the 76ers, who is not a bubbly, vivacious sort by nature. But this day he looked particularly somber, almost mournful. Kos never was one for small talk. He had a unique way of getting right to the heart of the matter.

And his first words to me as I stepped across the threshold were:

"Pat, I want you to meet your new owner."

Just like that.

Not even a perfunctory how-are-you good morning. Not even a gentle, "I've decided to sell the team."

Instead: *"Pat, I want you to meet your new owner."*

You have to admit that as an attention-getter, that's a beaut.

This was particularly shocking because there had been absolutely no hint that anything like this was in the works. We would learn later that all through the winter Kos had been locked in super-secret negotiations to sell the team he had owned since 1963. His own business interests had been accelerating and he was finding himself with less time for the team. His son, Ted, was not all that interested in devoting his time to the team. And Kos had suffered an ulcer attack a year earlier. So the sum of it was that here he was, close to seventy, and feeling that his life was intensifying instead of winding down.

But his decision to sell had not been a sudden whim. He had wrestled with it, agonized over it, and, in fact, only minutes before we walked through the door he had signed the papers making the sale official.

As Kos had dropped that Meet-Your-New-Owner bomb, he had nodded his head slightly. Taking that cue, I turned to my left, as Kos was saying: "This is Fitz Eugene Dixon."

It was a name all of us had heard many times. A man of extreme wealth. Heir to the vast Widener transportation fortunes. He had been part owner of the Philadelphia Flyers. He had had interests in the Phillies and the Eagles.

Anyway, here was this short, bespectacled man and he was fairly beaming, a positive glow of elation and glee radiating from him.

I managed to stumble out something like "Congratulations." Which he accepted, all the while vigorously pumping my hand and continuing to beam. Here was a man who was obviously pleased with himself and with what had happened.

The introductions continued then. Peter Mattoon, Dixon's attorney. Dixon's son George. Hello. How are you? Nice to meet you. My pleasure. And then: Hunter McMullin, a proper Main Line type, whose first words, dripping with smugness, were: "And when did *you* find out about the sale?" He knew, of course, that I had found out about the sale all of 30 seconds ago. The tension immediately turned several layers thick. It would set the tone for what would last several years.

By now, it was late in the morning, and a press conference had been called for 2 that afternoon in Mattoon's law offices. It went well. It was generally cordial. Except Peter Mattoon came up to me and whispered: "As long as you're with the 76ers, this is the last kind of press conference you'll attend." His meaning was clear—the team was solidly entrenched in the Dixon family now. I felt as if I'd been slapped across the face with a wet washcloth.

I had been through this before. I had been the general manager in Chicago and in Atlanta when the teams there were sold, and I would go through it again with the Sixers. But it's always traumatic. You never quite get used to: "Meet your new owner."

It was Memorial Day weekend, and that night I had dinner with Kos, and it was an emotional one. He tried to reassure me, said that I wouldn't have to worry about my job. This was a painful time for Kos because the team had meant so much to him. It was his hobby, his yacht, his radio station; he didn't dabble in other things the way many rich men did. His only outside interest had been the Sixers, and he was genuinely fond of the team. The letting go hurt a lot.

The next week Peter Mattoon and Fitz came to my office and said: "We want you to stay, to continue as GM. What kind of deal will it take?" I replied: "I'd like a few days to think about it." Later I met with Fitz and told him I'd like a five-year deal. It was agreed to in less than a minute.

As the 1975–76 season was nearing an end, there were reports that several ABA teams were about to fold. Now a few of the players in the ABA, including Moses Malone, had turned pro before their senior year, which meant they had not been drafted by the NBA. One such player was Melvin Bennett, a big, burly forward from the University of Pittsburgh who had gone to the Virginia Squires of the ABA. As the reports of the ABA's demise grew more widespread, the NBA Commissioner called an emergency draft so that those ABA players who still would have been in college could be drafted by NBA teams if their ABA employers went out of business. It sounds more complicated that it was, but the intent was to keep 18 NBA clubs from falling all over each other to sign Malone. Anyway, in that emergency draft, the Sixers took Mel Bennett. He was represented by a couple of New York attorneys, Louis Schaffel and Jerry Davis. They said their man wanted a five-year guaranteed contract from the Sixers at about $100,000 per year.

So my first act as Fitz Dixon's GM was to go to Fitz and tell him this was Bennett's demand. Fitz never hesitated. His reaction was: "Let's do it if you think we should." There would be some monumental consequences down the road. Mel Bennett would not contribute anything on the court, and, in fact, would be traded to Indiana in exchange for a first-round draft pick in 1980. And *that* would turn out to be a guard named Andrew Toney. It would be nice if you knew, in advance, that what seemed fairly innocuous at the time would, five year later, be one of the most fortunate deals you ever made.

Anyway, here comes the draft in June of 1976, and Gene Shue says that the Sixers need an offensive player. So we select Terry Furlow, 6–5 swingman from Michigan State who had led the Big 10 in scoring for two years. He had been touted to us by Jerry Krause, an old Chicago friend and a veteran baseball and basketball bird dog who was called "The Sleuth" in honor of his ability to uncover hidden talent. He had scouted Furlow for us while Jack McMahon had been laid up in the hospital with a bad back.

On the sixth round of the '76 draft, the Sixers took Mike Dunleavy, a guard from South Carolina, a tough Irish kid who had grown up in Brooklyn. At this stage of the draft we were, frankly, just taking bodies.

Now in the summer of '76, fresh off a winning season and encouraged despite that devastating playoff loss to Buffalo, the Sixers were busily engaged in preparing the advertising campaign for the 1976–77 season. For a long time, we had been using the Sonder Levitt Advertising Agency of Philadelphia. S&L had coined that "The 1976ers—The Team of the Year" slogan for the previous season, which had been hastily revised to "Let George Do It" once the Sixers acquired McGinnis. S&L had already prepared the campaign for the 1976–77 season, with two principal themes: "Buy the Seat You'll Never Sit In." And: "Stand Up for the Sixers."

There was a problem, however. Dixon's people wanted to employ a new agency, McDonald and Little, headquartered in Atlanta. They had used that agency during the short-lived box lacrosse league's existence, which had included the Philadelphia Wings, owned by Fitz Dixon. This campaign with the Sixers was going to involve hundreds of thousands of dollars. I was arguing that we should retain Sonder Levitt, and Dixon's people were adamant for McDonald and Little.

Fitz Dixon decided to resolve the dispute by holding a summit meeting at his mansion in Winter Harbor, Maine. Instead of coming to Philly to settle matters, he hired two private planes. We came to the mountain, two planeloads of advertising agency types and Sixers executives of varying rank and influence.

Fitz used a term we would hear more than once. "I'm taking the owner's prerogative," he said, "and we're using McDonald and Little."

End of dispute.

Except by late August, when we should have launched the advertising campaign for the new season, McDonald and Little haven't come up with anything and are obviously spinning their wheels. Fitz is upset and he calls another summit meeting, this one at his Pennsylvania farm.

"We made a mistake," said Fitz. "Get that other agency. We want them back."

It cost him $25,000 to buy out the deal from McDonald and Little.

So Sonder Levitt was back with the Sixers. But this was just the beginning of what would become a whole series of minor annoyances for the new owner, annoyances that would snowball and finally become one large lump of frustration. The next annoyance would be a larger one, and it involved the coach, Gene Shue. . . .

Just prior to the sale of the Sixers to Dixon, I had gotten a call from Richie Phillips, the Philly lawyer, who said: "I have been hired by Gene Shue to act as his agent. When can we get together to discuss his contract?

This was an unprecedented move at the time. No coach in the NBA had an agent in those days, let alone an attorney who was also serving as an agent for several players in the same league, as well as the same team. So now I had to go to the new owner and tell him his coach had hired the toughest player representative around.

Fitz took the news as a challenge, a personal one. His reaction was: "Oh, so they're trying to take advantage of the new kid on the block, huh?"

Kos, although he was no longer the owner, was equally infuriated. "If he [Shue] had done that to me, I'd have fired him on the spot," Kos snapped.

The Sixers hadn't yet assembled for training camp and already there was friction. Gene had elected to play hardball in an era when hardball wasn't fashionable for coaches, and he was going against an owner accustomed to getting his own way.

And guess who got caught in the middle, between a rock and a hard place? The general manager.

Fitz' position with me was: "You should be negotiating with the coach just as hard as you would with any player."

Gene's position with me was: "You should be standing up for me."

It got ugly.

Gene Shue and I had had a warm relationship. But it quickly grew cold. And our negotiating sessions were nasty, filled with

50

venom, legal pads and pencils being thrown around, ricocheting off the office walls. It became, eventually, intolerable. I finally had to go to Fitz and tell him this was one negotiation I was going to have to bow out of, that Gene felt I should be his ally and Fitz thought I should be working in his best interests. So Peter Mattoon represents Fitz and Richie Phillips represents Gene, and their negotiations grind on and on. They will finally reach an agreement in October, on opening day, and Fitz gives in and Gene ends up, at the time, the highest paid coach in basketball.

But the seeds of dissension have been planted and Gene is in a precarious position. As long as things go well, as long as this team wins, he will be okay. But if things turn sour, he has already backed himself into a corner. Gene and Fitz are like a couple of matchsticks, ready to burst into flame at the slightest provocation. They will co-exist, but it will be an uneasy truce.

As training camp begins for the '76–'77 season, there is eager anticipation once more. This has the makings of a good team. Doug Collins and George McGinnis are All-Stars and there is a solid supporting cast. Caldwell Jones has joined the team. The ABA has, as long predicted, folded that summer, with four of its teams—Denver, San Antonio, Indiana and New Jersey—being assimilated into the NBA. The Sixers had to pay $75,000 to the league office to assure themselves of acquiring Caldwell immediately without a legal battle. Fitz had paid that without blinking.

Now, on the eve of camp, there is a call from Barry Mendelsohn, the GM in New Orleans, about Henry Bibby, an experienced, smart guard who had been part of the UCLA collegiate dynasty. New Orleans needs cash. We strike a conditional deal that if Bibby can make the Sixers team by opening day, we get him and New Orleans gets $10,000. Fitz agrees again, and again does so instantaneously.

The only problem is that the Sixers' roster is too full. There is CJ and McGinnis and Collins and Dawkins and Free and Mel Bennett and now the rookie draftees, Furlow and Dunleavy, plus

Henry Bibby, and the other players from the season before. Henry Bibby will make the team, and will be a starter for almost four full seasons. But suddenly the Sixers have too many bodies . . . and just about this time comes a hint that they have a chance at the most heavenly body in all of basketball. . . .

After the merger, there are ominous rumblings from out on Long Island, home of the New York Nets, and also home of one Julius Erving. He is saying that the Nets' owner, Roy Boe, has made contractual promises that he is not fulfilling. Further, says Erving, if these promises are not kept, he will not report to camp.

Knowing it is the longest of long shots, I make a call to Billy Melchionni, who had been a great collegiate player at Villanova and who had remained in Philly to play for the Sixers. Now he is the general manager of the Nets.

"If things ever deteriorate to the point that you have to trade Julius Erving, please let us know," I tell Billy, and never really think any more about it. It was kind of like saying to Raquel Welch's mother, "Hey, if she ever needs a date, here's my phone number."

Julius Erving, true to his word, does not report to the Nets camp. His holdout is two weeks old when we get a call in the Sixers offices from Melchionni.

"We're willing to listen to what you have to offer for Julius," he says. "I'll tell you this: Roy Boe wants cash for him."

I swallow hard and ask: "How much?"

"Three million dollars."

Now that's not a bad attention-getter, either.

"You have my permission," said Billy, "to talk to Julius' agent. That's Irwin Weiner."

I went out to Fitz Dixon's office. The new owner had been the epitome of cooperation up to now. Every time we came to him and asked him to get out his checkbook, he had never hesitated. But $3 million. . . .

"Uh, Fitz," I began, "there is a player available from the other league." I paused for dramatic effect. I let the suspense build before I dropped this name on him.

"And his name," I continued, pausing once more, "is Julius Erving."

Then I leaned back triumphantly, expecting him to come right out of his chair in disbelief and delight. I was prepared for almost any reaction except the one I got.

Fitz leaned forward in his chair and said, quite earnestly: "Now tell me, Pat, who is he?"

Who is Julius Erving? You might as well ask, *who* is Enrico Caruso? *Who* is Shakespeare?

More than a little taken back, I stammer and say: "Uh, well, Fitz, he's kind of the Babe Ruth of basketball."

Fitz's favorite line is: "Fine and dandy." When he is pleased, when things are going well, it's: "Fine and dandy."

This time was one of those fine and dandy times.

"Now tell me, Pat, what has he done?"

Have you got a couple of weeks? I quickly dismiss any such snappy repartee, and straightforwardly begin listing the accomplishments of the single most exciting basketball player ever to levitate.

"Sounds interesting," says Fitz. "What do they want for him?"

For some reason, $3 million does not come trippingly to the tongue. But I manage to say it without fainting.

Fitz looks at me and narrows his eyes and asks, point-blank: "Are *you* recommending this?"

I gulp and say: "Yes, sir, I am."

"Fine and dandy, then. Let's do it."

We have one problem, however. How will the coach feel about this? You might assume that any coach would erupt in ecstasy at the chance of acquiring Julius Erving. But there is a fragile chemistry on a basketball team, and it doesn't take much to disrupt it, and when it is disrupted, then you can have all of the individual talent in the world but if it does not mesh together, it is doomed. Did Gene Shue feel that he could coach George McGinnis and Julius Erving on the same team? Could two stars of such magnitude co-exist? If he wasn't satisfied it would work, we weren't going to pursue Julius. Gene agonized over the decision for ten days.

Finally, I asked him: "What would be your reaction if Julius ended up with the Knicks?" With reservations, Gene became enthusiastic. He had a deep-seated hatred for the Knicks. So began the Erving chase.

It quickly became obvious that the Nets were shopping Julius Erving all over the league. The Sixers hardly had the inside track. This was going to be one of those sell-to-the-highest-bidder deals. Any thoughts we might have had that we were the only ones in the running quickly dissipated when the elevator door leading to Irwin Weiner's office opened and all the light was blotted out by this immense presence. It was Wayne Embry, 6–8, 300 pounds, a one-time pro basketball player and now the general manager of the Milwaukee Bucks. I knew he hadn't come to Weiner's office to talk about the price of popcorn.

But Weiner has some news that buoys us instantly. Julius Erving says he prefers to remain in the East. Philadelphia, he adds, is acceptable.

Once the initial elation passes, it is time to ask the multi-million-dollar question: How much will it cost the Sixers to sign Julius.

Weiner exhales a plume of blue cigar smoke and these figures: Half a million to sign. A salary of $450,000 per year for six years. Plus of course, $3 million to the Nets.

The grand total, then, makes Julius Erving the Six Million Dollar Man?

Irwin Weiner nods, indicating the math is correct.

There is another delicate situation to be handled. How will George McGinnis react to this? Playoff failure aside, he has been the cornerstone of the new Sixers. He had willingly consented to the immense burden of *Let George Do It*, and now he would be asked to share center stage. Knowing Julius Erving's flair and flamboyance, George also had to know that he would no longer be the only star. So I approached him and asked him how he felt, assuring him that if he were opposed we would not pursue Julius. Looking back, that put George in an absolute no-win position. Asking him how he felt about acquiring Julius was like asking that old question:

When did you stop beating your wife? If he said he was opposed, no way, man, well, if that ever got out, George would be crucified. If he agreed, gave his endorsement, he had to know he was shifting the spotlight off himself. Probably forever.

George seemed to be enthusiastic.

"If you can get Julius, then you've got to," he said.

In retrospect, George McGinnis was given a godfather offer; there was no way he could refuse, and there was no way he could win.

So the season is to start on Friday night, October 22, and on Wednesday, the 20th of October, at one-forty in the afternoon, Jack McMahon and I are sitting around in my office wondering if the phone will ever ring. We're still awaiting word from the Nets on our acceptance of their terms for Julius. The phone rings and it's Roy Boe and he starts with small talk, while my heart is beating like a triphammer. Finally, he says: "We have decided. . . ." There is a long pause. Here we are waiting for words for posterity and Roy Boe is milking the moment for its drama.

". . . to accept your offer."

I get an adrenalin rush you wouldn't believe and flash the thumbs-up sign to Jack, who would have turned cartwheels except he almost fell out of his chair. Just as Boe and I hung up, Fitz Dixon walked in.

"Fitz, we got *him*."

The owner beamed and rubbed his hands together and walked around in little circles, and he kept saying: "Wonderful . . . wonderful . . . oh my, that's wonderful. . . ."

A few weeks ago he hadn't even known who Julius Erving was and now he was beside himself.

There remained, of course, a ton of legal work to be completed before the Six Million Dollar Man was officially a 76er, and the new season was hardly 48 hours away. We all sped for New York, Peter Mattoon, Morris Cheston, Jr., another attorney, and myself. Mattoon and I headed south for Weiner's lawyers' office to meet the agent and Julius, while Cheston headed north for the Nets' lawyers' offices. At a little past two in the morning, Julius, having read and re-read every word in the contract, having examined every detail, affixed his signature to the contract. Then we all hustled over to the Nets' lawyers' offices to help Cheston. At six A.M. it had all been concluded.

Julius Erving was a 76er at last.

There was a press conference in Philly that evening, and it was the largest one in the city's history. That very day also happened to be the fourth wedding anniversary for Jill and me, and that night, on the way to a restaurant to celebrate, she casually drops this one on me:

"Are you ready to be a daddy again?"

She is expecting our second child the following June.

You might say those twenty-four hours had been fairly eventful.

The next night the 76ers opened the 1976–77 season at home in the Spectrum, against the San Antonio Spurs, and it was a happening.

Julius Erving, George McGinnis, Doug Collins, Lloyd Free, Darryl Dawkins, Caldwell Jones, Joe Bryant . . . a whole roster of marquee names. The Sixers are promptly dubbed "The Best Team Money Can Buy."

Julius is introduced and a fan comes running out of the stands to hand him one of those black bags doctors carried back in those days when they still made house calls.

There's only one problem. The Sixers lose.

They go to Buffalo the next night, and they lose again.

The Best Team Money Can Buy starts out 0 and 2.

The win column is empty but the roster is too full. Before the season began, we had to put Mike Dunleavy and Mel Bennett and Clyde Lee on the disabled list. Lee refuses, demands to be traded or released. Nothing can be worked out and, reluctantly, we have to waive him. We spend the next two weeks trying to accommodate Bennett, and finally trade him to Indiana, getting their first-round draft pick in 1980. That seems, at the time, an eternity away. When that pick turns out to be Andrew Toney, it will have been worth the wait.

The one player, during this hectic time, that the Sixers did not have to trade was Billy Cunningham. He had tried to come back from that knee injury, and had even reported to camp. But water kept collecting on the knee and he knew this was the end of the line. One night, just before we acquired Erving, just before the season was to open, Billy was sitting at home with his wife, Sondra, and he suddenly said: "I think I'll retire." Sondra looked at her watch and answered: "Yes, it is getting late. Me, too." And Billy had said: "No, no, that's not what I mean. . . ."

But there was another 76er who would be traded that winter.

Fred Carter.

He had been a loyal soldier, nicknamed "Mad Dog," who had been the lead guard through all of those lean years, including that 9–73 season. Freddie had been the one to take all the crucial shots during all of those dismal years, and it would have been nice if he could have concluded his career with a team that was now established as a winner. But the harsh fact was the Sixers simply had too many talented offensive players at this point. Fred was sitting more than he was playing and we tried to trade him for almost two months.

Finally, in December, Milwaukee got hit with injuries to its guards and was in trouble. They took Fred Carter and in exchange the Sixers received the Bucks' second-round draft picks for 1977 and 1978.

That deal, which seemed rather innocuous at the time, would turn out to be a largesse for Philadelphia. That is the strange thing about trades. Sometimes the ones you think will be blockbusters are nothing more than duds. And, occasionally, one you make and don't think much of at the time will develop into a bonanza down the road.

The Carter deal fell into the later category.

The second-round pick in 1977 turned out to be Wilson Washington, a forward from Old Dominion. He would not pan out in Philly and we would trade him, in turn, to the New Jersey Nets in exchange for future draft choices—second-round picks in '79 and '82, and a third rounder in '83. Well, the second rounder in '79 became Clint Richardson and the second rounder in '82 was Mitchell Anderson. And that second round pick in '78, courtesy of the Bucks for Fred Carter, became a quick guard from West Texas State named Maurice Cheeks.

Tracing the genealogy of a trade gets a little confusing, admittedly, but the sum and substance of dealing Fred Carter to Milwaukee was this: The Sixers would acquire two of their current players, Cheeks and Richardson, plus a third-round pick in 1983, and who knew what that might lead to.

Anyway, getting back to the 1976–77 season, The Best Team Money Can Buy righted itself after that 0—2 pratfall start. It would eventually win 50 games, lose 32, and win the division. It would also be the most closely chronicled team in NBA history. It was forever under the microscope, or on the shrink's couch. Everywhere that team went, there was an introductory press conference, featuring Julius Erving, and a sell-out.

It was a stunning collection of talent.

And controversy.

The roster had established stars and it had young, impetuous players. And it was a team that was the media's delight because almost everyone had something to say almost every night. Lloyd Free was proclaiming himself all-world. Not to be outdone when it came to hyperbole, Darryl Dawkins proclaimed himself to be all-universe. Joe Bryant was fighting with Steve Mix for more playing time, and popping off. Doug Collins was the emotional type to begin with. Terry Furlow was sitting on the end of the bench, miserable and collecting rust. And, of course, there was the continuing soap opera of Julius Erving and George McGinnis and could they co-exist? Not to mention Gene Shue, highest paid coach in the NBA, trying to harness all of this chaos and put together some semblance of a team. There must have been nights when he felt like he needed a whip and a chair.

The Sixers led the league in attendance on the road that season, and at home the average was up over 15,000 per game. The city was completely infatuated. Understandably so. Every game was an aerial circus and the post-game press conferences were media circuses, each one trying to top the other in jive-talk and outrageous claims.

It had been a long, long time since the city had a professional basketball team that was a 50-game winner. This one went into the playoffs and squared off against an old tormentor: The Boston Celtics.

It was a seven-game war, the Sixers winning the finale, at home, 83–77, and the late heroics were supplied not by Julius Erving nor George McGinnis but by Lloyd Free. The self-proclaimed Prince of Mid-Air just devoured the Celtics guards, throwing up those high, arching fire-bombs from way out.

The Sixers had finished first in the regular season and then survived against Boston and now they were into the Eastern Conference finals, against the Houston Rockets, and the memories of the previous year's trauma with Buffalo were fast fading.

The Rockets had a prodigy in the pivot named Moses Malone. The Sixers won that series, too, wrapping it up in Houston, when referee Jake O'Donnell called an offensive foul on Houston's John Lucas in the closing seconds. It was a hairline decision, on one of those very close plays in which the violation could go either way. Usually, you expect the home team to get the edge on those calls. But the Sixers got the judgment instead, and Jake was regarded as a courageous, fair-minded, gutsy, ultra-objective arbiter in Philly. In Houston, of course, he was regarded as a blind incompetent who had choked in a moment of stress. It's little wonder that those who make their living by officiating sports events always lament that they have the one job in which you are expected to be perfect your first day and then make steady improvement.

So now the Sixers are off and winging. They have a regular season title, they have beaten Boston and Houston, and they have arrived at the championship finals. Quite a turnaround from a team that, only four seasons before, had compiled the worst record in the history of the sport. Their opponents, the champs of the West, would be the Portland Trailblazers, who revolved around a red-headed redwood of a center named Bill Walton, noted pacifist, vegetarian and exquisite team player.

The Sixers, of course, are favored. They have been ever since back in October when they acquired Julius Erving. Those who already have conceded the world title to the Sixers have done so reluctantly, implying that it will be a shame and that a Sixers triumph is going to set back the idea of *team* play several eons. Philadelphia is described as the ultimate playground team, all improvisation, one that simply free-lances and has so much natural talent that it can play right past all the bickering and dissension that rages through the locker room.

Sure enough, the Sixers open the series at home and win the first two games. But in the second game, Maurice Lucas, the power forward of Portland, and Darryl Dawkins get into a tiff that looks like it will escalate into a world heavyweight boxing match. Lucas uncorks a mighty punch. It misses. That is, it misses Darryl but lands instead on Doug Collins, a fairly innocent bystander at the time. Lucas advances menacingly on Dawkins, who backs away. Dawkins cocks his fists and makes some impressive dance movements, but he also continues to retreat. Lucas continues to come forward, though hardly at a decisive gait. It is obvious that neither one really wants to duke it out with the other.

They are ejected, and Dawkins storms into the Sixers' locker room and takes out his rage and frustration on the interior decor, specifically the toilet. He rips off one of the doors from its hinges, and later tells the media he is disappointed in his teammates because none have come to his aid. All this team needed at that point, of course, was some more controversy.

It will not end in four straight now. The series moves out to Portland and the Blazers win both, easily. Julius is carrying the team and George is more pitiful than ever. His confidence is completely shattered by now. Every shot he takes threatens to splinter the backboard. Soon, he quits trying to take them, and is paralyzed when the ball is in his hands. It is sad to see, this truly talented player reduced to uncertainty.

Locked at 2-2 in games, the series returns to the Spectrum, and there is another embarrassing defeat. It ends in Portland in Game 6, and even that is turmoil, particularly tantalizing because the

Sixers get a final shot, trailing by two points. It will not fall.

The Sixers will find little sympathy. The Trailblazers are the toast of the country, and their triumph is interpreted as a vindication of team play. The Sixers are scornfully written off as "Phutile Philly." George McGinnis is hung out to dry in print. Only Julius Erving is spared, the rest of the team dismissed as selfish ball hogs who got precisely what they deserved.

Almost as soon as the team has limped back home, Gene Shue is in my office saying: "I don't want him on this team any more. Get him outta here!"

The object of his disaffection is George McGinnis.

Ironically, within the next few months, it will be Gene who leaves and George who stays. For a while, that is. . . .

We're on the phone every day trying to deal George, but of course everyone else has seen his second straight playoff collapse and they're not anxious to trade for him. Gene, snarling, accuses me of sabotaging things. I say: "Gene, I can't arrange a trade." And he shoots back: "Well, just waive him, then." That is a ludicrous demand, but the emotions are running a tad high at the moment.

Gene, of course, is fighting for his own life. He has had a zoo of a team to deal with all year, and he has had the owner on him like a shadow. Fitz Dixon has spent all of this money and he can't understand why he doesn't have a winner. At one memorable point during the season, after a loss in December at home to the Warriors, Fitz had walked into the press room, face red, arms crossed, foot tapping impatiently, and had said to Shue: "Well, Gene, what are your excuses tonight?"

This was not, as you might gather, a picture of total harmony.

The whole season had been a tumultuous one, and it had left nerves frayed and raw and exposed, like downed electrical wires after a violent storm. The tension hissed and crackled.

For all of its talent, this team was not loved across the length and breadth of the land. Maybe it was the whole idea of cornering the market that had alienated people. At any rate, the Sixers were perceived as too good, to the point that they were never the underdogs, and, as we all know, the American public rarely roots for the overdogs. Too, the image had not been helped along by the new owner, who came across publicly as cold and arrogant, all the worst attributes people routinely associate with wealth. He didn't further his cause by moving from the superboxes down to the floor, setting up shop under the basket nearest the Sixers' bench. And he hired a former Secret Service agent, Bob Babilino, who, with a phalanx of security types, gave Fitz a menacing-looking escort wherever he went in the Spectrum. Additionally, they would make fans detour around Fitz's seat so that he always had an unobstructed view of the court. This wouldn't go over anywhere, but especially not in Philadelphia, where sports fans cannot tolerate snobbery and have no use for power plays. You push them, and they push back. Fitz was regarded as high-handed and much too elitist. Secretly, there were more than a few people pulling for his team to lose.

I had not made the playoff trips to either Houston or Portland, not because of doubt, but because Jill was due to deliver our child any day. Right after the playoffs ended, on the night of June 9, 1977, I was attending a Baker League game in McGonigle Hall at Temple University, a little bandbox of a building. There was a phone behind one of the baskets. It had a cover over it and appeared, for all purposes, to be long out of use. But I happened to be walking past it—what are the odds on this?—and it rang. Having nothing better to do at the moment, I picked it up. It was Jill, with a terse and urgent message: "It's time to go to the hospital." The labor was a long, hard one. At eleven-thirty the next morning, June 10, Bobby Williams was born in the Burlington County (New Jersey) Hospital in Mount Holly. That was exactly an hour and a half before the collegiate draft was due to start. I watched my new son breathe for all of two minutes, and then rushed to Philly for the draft. We were hoping, of course, to salvage something from the ashes of a season that began on such a high note and ended in yet one more frustrating loss in the playoffs. So who did we get? Glen Mosley and Wilson Washington. The names probably ring very few bells, and rightly so. I've always thought I should have just stayed at the hospital. . . .

For the Sixers, that season, for all of its tease and agony, had one salvation. The regular season and the playoffs had demonstrated that every adjective-splattered anthem of praise that had been written about him before was true. Julius Erving was, indeed, all that had been advertised.

From there, we could still build. . . .

BENSON

Billy Cunningham, back with the 76ers, is still a relentless competitor in this 1975 backboard battle with Clifford Ray and Jamaal Wilkes (41) of the Golden State Warriors.

Doug Collins slashes through three Denver defenders and scoops up a shot between Dan Issel (44), Bobby Wilkerson and David Thompson (33). This was Billy Cunningham's home coaching debut in November of 1977.

Even chronically arthritic knees have never grounded Julius Erving. This drive occurred against Washington in 1976.

This is one rebound Moses Malone (right), then with Houston, didn't get. Rockets teammate, Robert Reid, pries the ball away from Doc and Caldwell Jones.

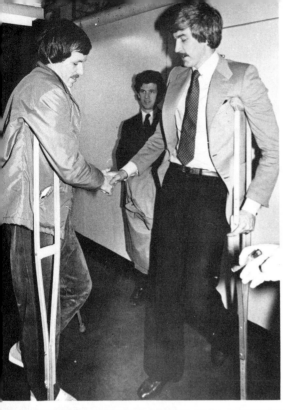

After one in a series of operations, Doug Collins (left) commiserates with another NBA veteran on crutches, Tom McMillen.

Near the end of a marvelous career, Walt Frazier finds himself in Cleveland, with the ball, and a hawking young Sixer, Lloyd (later to be World B.) Free.

GEORGE

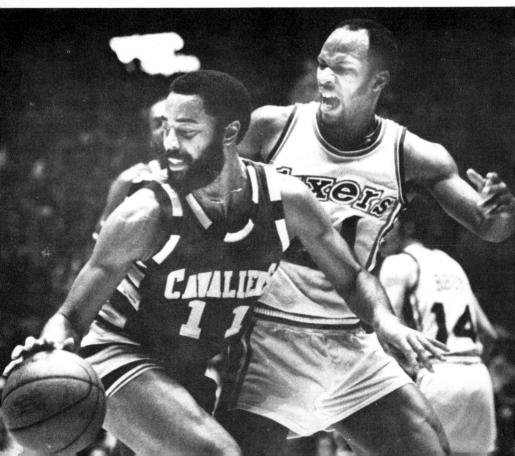

EORGE BILYK

The two most celebrated players to go directly to professional basketball from high school, Moses Malone and Darryl Dawkins, battle in a 1977 playoff game.

Steve Mix (50)
and Darryl Dawkins
sandwich Rudy
Tomjanovich of
Houston while
Moses Malone
pumps a jump shot.

A young Moses
Malone, then with
Houston, chases
Julius Erving,
Caldwell Jones and
Henry Bibby for a
loose ball.

I. GEORGE

Jewelry flying, Darryl Dawkins powers past Kareem Abdul-Jabbar in the 1980 NBA finals at the Spectrum.

Darryl Dawkins and Henry Bibby surround Moses Malone in the 1977 Eastern Conference finals.

Showing the same intensity and determination he displayed as a player, Billy Cunningham lectures the troops during a time-out in his first season as 76ers coach. Jack McMahon, right, and Chuck Daly, both valuable aides to Billy C., listen to the strategy.

Billy Cunningham opens the lines of communication in the locker room with Julius Erving and Joe Bryant (left).

Billy Cunningham's biggest challenge as the 76ers new coach in 1977 was motivating George McGinnis to play to his full potential, which, as this conversation suggests, was sometimes frustrating.

Wali Jones, who was a starting guard on the 1967 Sixers champions, ended up back in Philadelphia in 1976, and closed out his career. Jones now does some part-time scouting for the Sixers in Texas.

BENSON

I. GEORGE BILYK

Two of the Sixers' hard hats over the years, Steve Mix and Henry Bibby, scuffle with Houston's Robert Reid for the ball.

In one of the NBA's most famous playoff sequences, Doctor J curls under the backboard and levitates for a reverse layup despite the defensive attempts of Mark Landsberger and Kareem Abdul-Jabbar in the NBA finals of 1982 at the Spectrum.

The most familiar sight in professional basketball—Doc skying and slamming.

The savagery of the NBA finals of 1983 is graphically reflected in this collision between Maurice Cheeks of the 76ers and Jamaal Wilkes of the Lakers.

I. GEORGE BILYK

He called it "Mixville." It was that spot on the court where Steve Mix would either shoot a jumper or, in this case, back in for a push-hook. Defending are Larry Bird (33) and Chris Ford of Boston.

There is never unanimity of agreement about any official's call in an NBA game. Julius Erving and Steve Mix vociferously disagree with Bill Saar.

*Doc to Earth: Duck! Julius Erving stuffs thunder-
ously over Robert Parish of Boston while a grounded
Larry Bird watches in a 1982 playoff game.*

*Maurice Cheeks, who cracks the whip on the Sixers
fast break, slices past Kareem Abdul-Jabbar for a
layup in the 1983 finals.*

*Mike Mitchell of Cleveland uses a long reach to spear a rebound from Caldwell Jones while Steve
Mix is knocked aside.*

I. GEORGE

ORGE BILYK

Darryl Dawkins clears away Kareem Abdul-Jabbar while Doc does another skywalk in the 1980 NBA finals.

The Sixers' mascot, Big Shot, gets Spectrum fans into the act at an early age.

Harvey Pollack, the Sixers' Super Stat.

The brain trust of the world champions—Matty Guokas (left), Jack McMahon and Billy Cunningham.

4

Doc

JULIUS WINFIELD ERVING II.
The Doctor.
Dr. J.
Doc.

If the Dallas Cowboys are, as they proclaim themselves to be, America's Team, then I'm not so sure the 76ers might not be the World's Team.

And all because of one player, one man. Julius Erving.

On a global scale, certainly the most recognized athlete of all time is Muhammad Ali. Probably a notch below him is Pele, soccer being such a big international sport. And Doc, in terms of recognition, is probably right behind the boxer and the soccer player. He is known and revered on almost every continent by millions of people who have never seen him play. The only country I've ever visited where Doc was just another face was China. But should they ever rig a basket on the Great Wall, then he'd be bigger than chopsticks there, too.

We get mail in the Sixers' office from all around the country,

65

from all over the world, and there is one common thread of sentiment running through it all—people write to say they're pulling for us to win a championship because they feel that Doc deserves it. They want him to have the championship ring before he retires. Their emotion seems to be that this would be the capper for his grand career, that it would be only fitting.

Doc is 6 feet 6 inches tall but he stands much higher than that in the public's eye because they have put him on a pedestal.

All this adulation starts, of course, with Julius Erving the player. He has the long, lithe body of a greyhound; his physique is elastic, and he can coil, explode in a bounding leap, then recoil. His arms are inordinately long and, like telescopes, they seem to be able to stretch out as he wills them. His greatest physical assets, however, are his hands. From pinky to thumb, they measure 11 inches. To visualize that, picture a standard piece of typing paper, 8½ inches by 11 inches. Doc could put his thumb on the bottom left corner, stretch out his fingers, and his little finger would be touching the top righthand corner of the page. You shake hands with Doc, and everything from your elbow down gets swallowed up. For him, a basketball is no larger than a tennis ball. So he can handle the ball with one hand, with ease, and this leaves him all the rest of his considerable body and mind to concentrate on other things.

Like flying.

It is in an open court, when both teams are out and running, that Doc is the most effective and the most entertaining. He has this graceful, bounding, loping stride that gobbles up ground in huge gulps. More than once, we have seen him get the ball at mid-court, take *one* dribble, and end up with a slam-dunk. You watch this and you are convinced they have repealed the laws of gravity.

The sport of hang-gliding must have been inspired by the sight of Doc flying and jamming.

By his own admission, much of what Doc does is instinctive and improvised. Off the court, he is deliberate, methodical, selective. On the court, however, he simply gives himself over to his imagination and that marvelous inner gyroscope that steers him

66

through time and space.

"It seems like I've always been able to jump and dunk," he said. "It just happened; it wasn't anything I ever planned. It was a gift I accepted as a matter of course, and it wasn't until I got older that I ever bothered to analyze it, question it."

He went to the University of Massachusetts and immediately began to do outrageous things with a basketball. A writer who covered U-Mass at the time remembers getting a phone call from another basketball writer, and the conversation went something like this:

"Tell me about that young Jewish kid, that Julius Erving."

"Well, for starters, I don't think he's Jewish."

"How come?"

"He's black, for one thing. And for another, I'm not sure he's not from another planet. I saw him make some moves that aren't supposed to be humanly possible."

"So why don't you write about them?"

"I'm not sure anybody would believe me."

It took the camera to convince people, and even today Doc is capable of an occasional sortie around the rim that will merit four or five consecutive slow-motion replays, with the announcer finally asking: "How does he do that?"

Doc himself isn't always sure.

"I'd say, 95 percent of the time something I've done on the court I can remember doing previously," he said. "But every once in a while I'll do something, and afterwards, running down the court, I'll think, 'Hmmmm, I don't ever recall *that* one before.' "

So what, exactly, is the sensation of flying without wings?

"Nothing I can describe," he said. "It happens so fast, there's no time for evaluation. Most of it is subconscious. Or unconscious. Sometimes I'll watch a video replay and reflect on a particular move, but I can't recall what I was thinking at the time."

He has had to make one concession to age.

"When I was younger," he agreed, "I'd just do it and think about it afterwards. Now there seem to be more occasions when I think about what I'm going to do *before* I do it. I know there will

67

come a day when I'll think about a move and won't be able to do it. That is inevitable."

It is one thing to have immense physical talents, it is quite another to utilize them, to be a wise caretaker of them. So often in this business you see athletes who have been blessed with speed and size and strength, but they are profligate spendthrifts. They don't take care of themselves and they burn out quickly and they end up bitter, feeling that their bodies betrayed them, when all along it was the other way around.

Life expectancies in professional sports are notoriously short; athletes have a sort of half-life. Yet Julius Erving has been playing pro basketball since the fall of 1971. That's 12 full seasons, five in the old ABA, seven in the NBA, which puts him right up there with the gray-beards in this sport. Twelve years add up to an awful lot of take-offs, and, more important, an awful lot of landings. Remember that Doc has chronically arthritic knees, to which he straps ice bags after each game. So he has managed to make a lie of all the actuarial charts and, surprisingly, this past season, at the age of 33, he seemed friskier, bouncier, more alive than ever. Getting Moses Malone helped because that freed Doc from some of the hugger-mugger around the basket. Doc didn't have to go in there trying to dig out every rebound, and he could spend his energy and effort in some other areas, do a little more orchestrating; in fact, he probably became a better all-around player this season. Billy Cunningham says Doc's passing has never been better and his defense is the best it's been in his career.

None of this is by accident. Doc works in practice. He sets the tone, the tempo. A lot of superstars' work habits are atrocious, but Doc has always given completely of himself, and his attitude is contagious. Every team takes its cue—in practice, in attitude, in play—from its leader, and Doc is the Sixers' leader. The noticeable lack of locker room cliques and dissension is due in large part to him.

Too, Doc takes none of his physical gifts for granted. He is a jealous, zealous preserver of them. The Sixers' trainer, Al Domenico, says: "If Doc gets a pimple, he wants a biopsy taken, he wants it analyzed, he wants to know why it's there and how to get rid of it." He is concerned almost to the point of hypochondria, but it's refreshing to see a man so skilled who realizes what he has, appreciates it, and goes to such lengths to protect it.

From the day we first acquired Doc, we have lived with the pressure of being expected to win it all, or the season is regarded as a failure. I still remember the press conference at which Julius was introduced as a Sixer. The coach at the time, Gene Shue, asked: "Am I allowed to lose even one game?" It was asked jokingly, but there was a certain apprehension there, a realization that, no, he wasn't allowed to lose even one, not with the most exciting player in the game now on the team. It was a burden of great expectations we all took on ourselves.

But then Doc has been lugging that load around ever since he first laced on sneakers, went climbing into the clouds, sending messages like: "Doc to Earth . . . Doc to Earth . . . Duck!"

And now we're getting into another, a more important area, which is Doc the man, the person, the manner in which he has responded to all this pressure. He has done so with grace and dignity, with style and flourish, and with amazing resiliency and responsibility.

You see so many gifted players who refuse to spend themselves. They sign a megabucks, guaranteed contract, and it's as though the ambition drains right out of them. They become indifferent, uncaring, and their effort is sporadic at best.

Not Doc.

He realized early on that he owed something to his public. Ever since he joined the Sixers, we have led the league in attendance on the road almost every year. Almost every game away from Philadelphia is a full house, and Doc is the man who fills those seats. Ticket buyers will line up in front of a team's box office, get to the window, plunk down their money, and say simply: "Gimme two for The Doctah." The home team may lose to the Sixers, but the outcome is incidental. If the fans have seen Doc skywalking, if they have seen another acrobatic finger roll, another tomahawk stuff, then they go away into the night happy and satisfied and contented. They have seen Dr. J, and the memory will carry them over until the next season.

Doc is acutely aware of this, knows that he is never allowed to have an off night. The people don't care if this is the fourth game in five nights in a fourth different city; they want to see Doc do something spectacular. He never disappoints them. Still, that is one monstrous load to carry, to know that people have come only to see you, that they are expecting you to deliver something special, expecting you to play each game as though it were your last. Doc does. And he never complains. He has the perspective to understand that such responsibility goes with the territory.

He said it was all brought home to him at a family reunion a few summers back. Doc was introduced to a distant relative, a man who happened to be a minister, and the man said to him: "The Lord done laid a mighty big blessing on you, Julius."

People consider it a privilege, you see, to be able to watch Doc play. The only other athlete I can remember facing that was Joe DiMaggio. Whole families would come to see him, knowing they might never see such grace again. That is, indeed, a mighty big blessing. Also, a mighty big challenge.

It is human nature to resent such a blessing, and yet to be frightened by it. But over and over, I have heard Doc tell writers how there comes a time when "you have to dare to be great." In other words, you lay it all on the line and forget, for the moment, the consequences of possible failure.

Failure, after all, isn't not succeeding. Failure is not taking the chance, not making the effort, not trying.

Of all the big-name athletes, Doc is the only one I've met who is completely without airs. You never have to hold your breath about what he's going to say for public consumption or how he's going to conduct himself. His deportment, his manners, his lifestyle are impeccable. He is very perceptive about people, as though he has these little invisible antennae that pick up on the emotions of the moment. He has a special warmth about him; he is kind, attentive. This doesn't mean he doesn't have an ego, or that he isn't vain. Everyone who is creative does, and you only have to watch

70

Doc make one trip down the floor to know that he is a creative genius with a basketball.

But there is no swaggering strut about him, no false bravado, no gaudy quotes, no self-aggrandizing braying. You don't see Doc brandishing a fist or threatening to duke it out with another player or yammering at his teammates. Most of the time he plays with an expressionless face, an aura of almost casual nonchalance. He has become, with age, a smarter player, more economical, better able to do more with less wasted energy. He has learned to husband his resources and his skills. But never does he waste emotion on the frivolous. If you see the suggestion of anger clouding Doc's face, that is unusual. Normally, he is placid, mellow, off the court; on the court, he is businesslike, almost deliberate and studied in his efforts to remain emotionless.

And yet he cares mightily about the image he projects, and he works at it. He is a cooperative, accessible interview, poised and patient, and as a consequence, he is a favorite of the media. They flock around his locker after every game, knowing he is the elder statesman, the team spokesman, and they will press him for analysis and interpretation. He talks in a soft, deep voice, always expansive, always offering more than one-word answers, choosing his words carefully. Veteran writers like to tell the story of one inquisitor talking to Erving just as a phone rang nearby. The inquisitor interrupted Doc to answer the phone, saying: "Hold that cliche, Doc, I'll be right back." But the point is, like everything else, he works at it. "You writers choose your words carefully," he says, "so why shouldn't I?" In college, he would have friends listen in on his interviews so they could critique him later, in private. As a result, Doc is smooth and polished before microphones and tape recorders. You never hear any mumbling from him, any stumbling, or a succession of "you-know's." He has worked at making himself articulate.

"When I see players today on TV and they struggle to get out a simple sentence," said Doc, "it makes me cringe. I know it doesn't have to be that way. Somewhere along the line, people took advantage of that person. They put him in a position where he was going to have to be a spokesman, and then gave him no training for it. He was used; he was just a piece of meat. So I disagree with coaches who want to shield a player from the media. It's okay to protect him for a while, providing you're using that time to develop him, preparing him for what he'll have to face. But if you're just milking him for his talent, then you're guilty of a greater sin than he is."

Doc, as you can see, is a sensitive person, very aware. Like a good many professional athletes, he grew up in the projects; in Doc's case, on Long Island. Sports was a way out. It was the escape route. Today, Doc lives in a mansion in Villanova on the Main Line. He has a lovely wife, Turquoise, and they have four delightful children. But Doc still remembers his roots, and he is properly grateful.

"Sometimes," he said, "I feel like I was born to play basketball. I've known a lot of people who worked just as hard, just as long, to develop the same skills I did, and yet it's not there for them. So I accept what I have as a gift. And I don't take it for granted. I feel you should be a steward of that which has been given to you, and remember that what can be given can also be taken away.

"I think I've got the best job in America. If I wasn't doing this for a living, I'd probably be playing the game a couple of nights a week at a "Y" somewhere, and I'd end up with all those bumps and bruises for free. Sure, the season is long and you take a beating. But then I always remember there are 250 million people in this country and there are only 250 players in the NBA. That makes you one in a million. Those are awesome numbers."

It is this sort of perspective that makes Doc so generous with his time. The Special Olympics. The March of Dimes. Lupus Foundation. American Dental Association. Police Athletic League. Hemophilia Foundation. Pennsylvania Adult Education. For all of these and dozens more charities and worthy causes, Doc is spokesman, adviser, endorser, honorary chairman. And it's all on the cuff. He does all these for free.

In 1969, when Doc was a freshman at the University of

Massachusetts, his older brother, Marvin, died from Lupus, one of the diseases Doc fights the hardest. The loss of his brother devastated him. It sent him into fits of weeping and mourning, and it had a profound effect on his personal philosophy.

"That was probably the first time in my life I ever felt completely powerless," he said. "Up to then, I had felt there wasn't anything I couldn't do. Playing basketball was like I had a license to fly. Then, when my brother died, so suddenly, without any warning, I realized how temporary that gift was. It changed a lot of my perspectives. I guess I do a lot of public service spots out of a sense of debt."

Doc isn't a particularly mercenary person. Nor is he a materialist. But he is one athlete who will not end up out on the street, busted and broke. He's very shrewd about his finances. He's surrounded himself with good advisers, sharp people, and he's expanded into other areas. When Julius Erving, basketball player, retires, then J. W. Erving II, entrepreneur, will take over. I'm confident it will be a smooth, successful transition. He's a wealthy man and he will become wealthier.

But he doesn't flaunt what he's got. There's no snob in him, none of that *nouveau riche* pretense. He's still very caring. I guess the one example that sticks out in my mind is the summer of 1981. We had just finished negotiations with Doc, signed a new contract, and I asked him, strictly as a personal favor for me, if he would give me one day and come to a basketball camp I was running in New York. He said sure, no problem. That day came and Doc was out in Denver. He had to fly most of the night into New York City and then transfer to a small commuter flight to Albany. He got there around noon, changed into basketball clothes, and went out there, under a hot summer sun, and worked all afternoon with 500 kids on blacktop basketball courts, and he never lost any of his patience, kindness or enthusiasm. That is what is so impressive about the man: his willingness to give of himself.

Doc is very introspective. He believes in predestination and feels that he is merely acting out a script that was written a long time ago. We have talked about this frequently. Doc became a born-again Christian a few years ago, and it changed his life. It's the sort of thing he's quite willing to share, but only if you ask him about it. By that, I mean he's not a vocal evangelist who "pushes" religion on people.

Doc believes that the Lord has a plan for all of us and that man is given a choice.

"But we should try to entwine our will with the will of our Creator," he said, "and put ourselves on the same road as His destiny for us. I was going on 30 before all of these pieces started to come together. But now there is a lot less confusion in my life. I had played basketball for a living for nine years and I was successful, I seemed to have fulfilled all my goals, but I still felt a void, like something was missing. It was a gnawing feeling that chewed at me. I guess I indicated how I felt to some writers and my thoughts appeared in print, and I started getting a lot of mailm People wrote to tell me the reason I felt this void was because Jesus Christ was missing from my life.

"I had finished the 1979 season depressed. For the first time in my career I had been seriously hurt. It was a severely pulled groin muscle, and it got me to thinking about my mortality, about how fragile my playing career really was."

That summer, Doc attended a family reunion. There were more than 300 of his relatives there, and he knew very few of them. most of them were from his father's side of the family; Doc's parents had separated when he was 3 years old, and his father had died when he was 9. So he didn't know any of those people, but of course they all knew him, by reputation at least. The talk revolved around the Erving family history, and Doc learned that it had been traced back to 1867 and was filled with religious overtones. Many of his ancestors had been deacons and pastors. It was about this time that the pastor laid that heavy line on Doc: "The Lord done laid a mighty big blessing on you, Julius."

That struck something in Doc.

"After that," he said, "I began to ask myself a lot of questions, and I wondered why I was one of the chosen, one in a million. Why should I be different? Why should I be different even from my peers? I practiced eight hours a day, and so did they, but why was I allowed to do things they weren't? I wanted to accept it as something that just came naturally, never question from where, or why. But I could no longer avoid wondering where such a gift came from. I made a commitment then; I asked the Lord to come into my life."

After that, Doc said he found a certain peace, a tranquility. It was, he said, as if he had at last found the path that had been intended for him all along.

And then he made another startling discovery: If he had found that path earlier in his life, there probably never would have been a Doctor J.

This is the way he put it:

"If I had committed myself to Christ when I was, say, 12 years old, I would probably be a missionary in Africa at this very moment, and there never would have been a Julius Erving, basketball player."

It's probably selfish to say this, and maybe even a little blasphemous, but for those of us who have been privileged to watch Julius Erving, basketball player, we are thankful he didn't make that discovery until later in his life. The world would have missed out on a whole lot of thrills.

And, besides, Doc has always been more than just a basketball player.

5

We Owe You One

BEING WORLD'S CHAMPION means never having to say you're sorry.

Unfortunately, the 1976–77 76ers never did realize what everyone believed to be their manifest destiny. That team was the NBA's version of Barnum and Bailey in sneakers. Step right up, see the Bearded Lady, the Tattooed Man, the Two-Headed Calf. As a box office attraction, it was without peer, the biggest road attraction in the league history. In 41 road games, those Sixers drew 632,994; they had 33 sell-outs away from Philadelphia, and nine more in the playoffs.

They had done everything but win the title. And now, in the summer of 1977, the disappointment was bitter and deep. After blowing that 2–0 lead against Portland and succumbing, gallingly, in four straight, they were not exactly heroes in their own city. Fitz Dixon's first year as owner had been an eventful one, albeit a crashing letdown. The failure in the playoffs was basketball's *slam-dunkus-interruptus*, and the city was angry, let down, frustrated. Expectations had been high ever since the acquisition of Julius Erving the autumn before. And now people were venting their passion, saying that Portland's victory had been a vindication for the purist's approach to the game, that Jack Ramsay's masterful team concepts had triumphed over Gene Shue's one-on-one circus. A *team* would beat a collection of All-Stars everytime, and it was as though some long-preached truth, some great fundamental, had been proven correct. To his credit, Fitz Dixon handled it well. "We were right in getting Julius," he said, "and I'd make the same decision a hundred times."

We met early that summer with the creative people from the advertising agency, Jerry Selber and Vic Sonder, and tried to brainstorm this dilemma. How do you pick up the pieces? How can you re-sell the team? They came back to us in July with a proposed theme that combined an apology with a promise: we're sorry, we blew it, and now we owe you one. We're not going to quit; we're coming back and we'll wipe out all those ugly memories.

So that became the slogan: We Owe You One.

It was unique. Professional teams don't go around publicly apologizing to their city. And they don't, as a common practice, do something as risky as putting it in terms of an IOU, a debt, a promissory note.

The Sixers spent half a million dollars on that campaign. It started out innocently enough. It would, of course, become a mocking boomerang.

Julius Erving was the logical choice as spokesman. So Doc did the radio spots and the TV spots, closing his locker door, turning slowly, deliberately to the camera, and saying in a calm purposeful voice: "We . . . owe . . . you . . . one," with dramatic pause between each word. Then he raised one large index finger. If you judge an advertising campaign on the basis of its impact on the public's memory, this one was an all-timer. People still remembered it, six years later.

The billboards over all of the city's expressways were plastered with the same slogan, highlighting one large index finger. Nobody ever knew this at the time, but that finger did not belong to Julius Erving. Doc was out of town when the photograph was taken, so the Sixers scouted around for the next largest index finger they could find. It belonged to a Baker League player named Ty Britt. And that was his digit, not Doc's, on the billboards.

78

During the summer of '77, the Sixers had to face two underlying problems in addition to recouping a city's affections, and both of those involved Coach Gene Shue. Gene had the patience of Job. He had made his reputation, first with the Baltimore Bullets and then with the Sixers, as a master of reclamation projects. He could take every other team's cast-offs, rejects and discards, and work magic with them. He could take the junkyard of the NBA and make it competitive and, ultimately, a winner. For one thing, he was, and is, a very good coach. For another, he could put up with about anything in terms of player eccentricities. But George McGinnis had worn him down. He came into the new Sixers' offices, which had been built from a warehouse complex inside Veterans Stadium that summer, and reiterated his demand that George be unloaded. "I don't care if we wind up getting nothing for him," he said, in total exasperation.

George was still corner-cutting. He would sneak out into the hallways in the middle of practice for a cigarette. During practices in the midst of the playoffs, he was wallowing in such a horrible slump, his confidence riddled, that even his own teammates were yelling "Brick!" when he put up a shot. There were a lot of young, impressionable players on the team and Gene feared they would follow George's lead and lapse into the same sort of poor work habits. Still, the Sixers were understandably reluctant to dump McGinnis at this point in time. His market value, after two wretched playoffs, was at its lowest point. That value needed to be resurrected first. Plus, we still owed George about a million and a half, and that was a lot of salary to eat.

Back in June, Gene had said: "Let's get rid of George—and the player I want is Bobby Jones."

Jones was with Denver at the time, a perennial member of the All-Defense team, and a genuine All-Star. I went so far as to call Carl Scheer, the GM of Denver, about a George-for-Bobby trade, and Carl just laughed. Neither one of us knew it then, of course, but almost a year to the day later we would be making that very swap.

The relationship between Gene and me had completely

79

deteriorated by then. I called Fitz and asked him to meet with Gene and explain the folly of trying to get rid of George at this time. Fitz doesn't like those kinds of meetings, and Gene can be very intimidating. But Fitz agreed to it, and then, greatly relieved, called me later to report that Gene had agreed to drop his demands. George McGinnis would remain with the Sixers for the coming season.

There was another problem, a touchy one, involving Gene and a woman, and it surfaced that spring. When Fitz found out about it, he was tempted to pull the plug on Gene. Fitz's background, breeding and temperament would not tolerate the slightest hint of indiscretion. Also, remember that he and Gene had been at each other's throats during Gene's salary negotiations. Fitz went so far as to ask me for a list of possible coaches. I prepared one, containing the names of some assistant coaches in the NBA, some collegiate coaches, and a few ex-players. One of the names on the list was Billy Cunningham.

Training camp opened that fall, with essentially the same team that had reached the finals and was now saddled with the demands of We Owe You One. One player did not survive the camp. Terry Furlow, an emotional, enigmatic sort, who had been the twelfth man on a twelve-man roster, got into a shouting, almost-shoving match with Jack McMahon. We had to get rid of Furlow or the last vestiges of discipline would have been hopelessly undermined. I managed to track down Bill Fitch, who was then head coach and general manager in Cleveland, and dangled Terry Furlow in front of him. Fitch asked: "What would you want for him?" I threw out the most outlandish terms I could think of: "Well, Bill, we'd need two No. 1 draft picks." He never even hesitated. "Yeah, I'd do that," he said.

So the Sixers got, for Furlow, Cleveland's No. 1 draft selections in 1981 and 1983. At the time, they were four years and six years down the road, and in sports, or life for that matter, you rarely think that far ahead. You put them in the bank and forget about them. We would end up spending those two draft picks by trading them to other teams. And what did we get in return? The first one brought us Lionel Hollins. The second one was partial payment for Moses Malone. So that phone conversation with Bill Fitch turned out to be immensely profitable. It would also, unfortunately, be tinged with tragedy. Terry Furlow would play for Cleveland, Atlanta and Utah, and then later be killed in an auto accident.

Camp concludes and the 1977–78 season starts, the season of promised atonement, the pay-back year, the cashing-in of We Owe You One.

What is supposed to be a crusade becomes, instead, an immediate bail-out. This is a full-scale retreat, a limping march to the rear. There is an uneasiness on the team. The players seem unsettled. Something is not right and it is obvious in their play. Perhaps they have lost respect for their coach. Whatever the reasons, the Sixers lose four of their first six games. The season is barely two weeks old and already the taunts have begun: We Owe You *Two*.

Fitz Dixon is furious. He has had enough. That fourth defeat is at home, against a not-very-good Chicago team, and the Sixers look pathetic. Fitz has been entertaining some friends and business associates before the game that evening. As the team deteriorates before his eyes, he suddenly stands up, under the basket, in full view of everyone in the Spectrum, and begins wig-wagging hand signals to his attorney and to me, motioning that he wants a summit meeting as soon as the game is over, and making menacing gestures in the direction of Gene Shue.

We gather in the lounge, as directed, afterwards, and Fitz is fuming.

"I've had it! I want that man out of here. Now. Who can you get to coach this team?"

My response is that the only logical person to turn to at this point in time is Billy Cunningham. He is still close to the players; he was the teammate of most of them, and he has their respect because they remember what a ferocious competitor he was. Plus, Billy C is extremely popular with the people of Philadelphia and the media, and that will help offset some of the backlash from the abrupt firing of Gene Shue.

Fitz says to proceed. Get Billy Cunningham.

Billy had been doing color commentary for CBS-TV, and doing very well. He had been at the game that night, and I phoned him at home around midnight and set up a breakfast meeting for the next morning. We got together at 10:30, in the downtown hotel of which he was a part-owner, and I thought to myself at the time that not too many people are interviewed as potential coaches while they're sitting in the building they own a piece of. Anyway, by noon, he wanted the job. We worked on the contract all afternoon, and we also tried to track down Gene Shue. We were told he was in Cleveland, scouting, but they had no record of him there, and every place we called in Cleveland we came away empty. The story broke that night. A press conference was set for the next morning, and ten minutes before it was to begin, we got hold of Gene Shue. By then, of course, he knew he was gone. The conversation was crisp and cool. The press conference was hot, as expected, but Billy's popularity was, indeed, a mitigating factor.

That was a Friday morning, and the Sixers were scheduled to play the New Jersey Nets, in Piscataway, that night. Billy's first game as new coach, and he hadn't even had time for a practice, barely had been introduced to the team, in fact. George McGinnis, always testing, forever stretching the limits, showed up at the team bus exactly one minute before it was due to pull out. Welcome to the Sixers, Billy.

His coaching debut is a successful one. The Sixers win, and it is close, hard-fought, and the big plays down the stretch are made by Darryl Dawkins. The big center had not gotten all that much playing time under Gene, who preferred experience and used Harvey Catchings and Caldwell Jones primarily in the middle. But Billy felt he had a big hoss in Darryl and he was going to ride him. Billy was demonic on the bench, sweating clear through his three-piece suit, hopping and jumping and whistling that shrill Brooklyn whistle that stopped the players dead in their tracks.

His excitement and commitment were just what that team

needed. It had become blase, laid-back, too nonchalant for its own good. Billy turned the pilot light back on and fanned it into a roaring blaze. He coached like he had played, all-out. From the bench, he dribbled every dribble, made every official's call, tried to go after every rebound. But his passion was contagious, and it seemed to spill over onto the team. Reawakened now, the Sixers returned home the very next night, before a sell-out crowd, and routed a very good Denver team. The crowd went bonkers. So did Billy. The Sixers could have sold his seat because he was rarely in it. Indeed, one game that season, he exploded off his chair so suddenly, so violently, that he split the seat right out of his trousers.

Billy was smart enough to realize that enthusiasm wasn't enough. He knew he needed help with the X's and O's. It wasn't that he didn't know the game, but now he was immersed in it from an entirely different vantage point. The perspective of a coach is not that of a player. He wanted to keep Jack McMahon, of course, because Jack is a piece of the rock, steady, reliable, and he's seen it all, experienced it all. But Billy wanted another assistant, too, someone well schooled in the intricacies and the subtleties of strategy and tactics. He got Chuck Daly, who had done such a marvelous coaching job at the University of Pennsylvania. This was early November, 1977, and Penn was about to start its own season, but, fortunately, Chuck had a very capable assistant himself in Bob Weinhauer, who replaced him.

The Sixers of 1977–78 won 55 games, lost 27. It was a five-game improvement in the won-loss column from the year before. It was, in fact, one of the most successful years in the history of the franchise. After that 2–4 start, the team finished 53–23 under Billy, who had furnished precisely the volatile spirit that was needed. Doc was brilliant as usual. Doug Collins had another All-Star type of season. Caldwell Jones was his usual quiet efficiency. Darryl Dawkins, getting more playing time, unfurled some awesome evenings. Even George McGinnis seemed to be reborn. And Lloyd Free had blossomed into a great clutch shooter.

The Sixers won their division and were rewarded with a bye in the first round of the playoffs. They met the New York Knicks in the second round and dismantled them in four straight.

The Kangaroo Kid had the team playing frenzied basketball.

It looked, now, like We Owe You One was going to be repaid, and with interest.

In the Eastern Conference finals that spring, the Sixers met the Washington Bullets, and the scenario couldn't have been more favorable. The Bullets hadn't even been expected to qualify for the playoffs. The consensus was they were living on borrowed time, were very fortunate to have survived this deeply into the playoffs. While the Sixers, with all that talent, rekindled by Billy C, were riding all sorts of momentum.

That Washington team had Wes Unseld, who jumped about two inches off the floor but was a voracious rebounder; and Elvin Hayes, whose one weapon was a turnaround jumpshot, which everybody knew was coming but still couldn't stop; and Kevin Grevey and Bob Dandridge, and the coach was Dick Motta, the feisty, fiery pepperpot. Destiny was in the midst of a rapturous love affair with those Bullets. They were going to be one of sports' miracle teams, one of those enchanted groups from whom little is expected and all they do is win a world championship. It happened to be the fate of the luckless Sixers to catch them at precisely the worst possible time. This would be the spring when the Bullets would keep escaping and Dick Motta would come up with one of the most memorable battle cries ever. Each time Washington's situation seemed hopeless, Motta would remind them, and everyone else, that it's never over 'til it's over. Or, in his words: "The opera ain't over 'til the fat lady sings."

The fat lady hit a high C against Philly, and it was the Sixers who shattered like glass.

The very first game of the series, in the Spectrum, is won by Washington, in overtime. The Sixers manage to win the second game, but now the homecourt advantage has been squandered. Elvin Hayes is devouring George McGinnis, and then taunting George about it in the papers. Bob Dandridge is giving Doc fits. The series moves to Washington, to the Capital Centre, for the weekend, and the combustible crowd urges on their team, par-

84

ticularly Hayes, the Big E. Every time he touches the ball, the crowd is shrilly crooning: "E-E-E-E-E-E-E!" The Sixers are positively undressed in both games, and stagger back home, down 3–1.

The team has now moved its practices out to Widener University, in suburban Chester, because this is Fitz Dixon's adopted alma mater. At one practice, with the team hanging by its fingernails, Lloyd Free comes to Billy and says he can't play anymore. The timing was hardly propitious. Lloyd had opened a shoe store in Philly, Lloyd's Free Throw; it is failing and he is close to bankruptcy, worried that his agent is milking him dry. He has everything except basketball on his mind. Billy has a long talk with Lloyd and convinces him to stay around and play. He does, and the Sixers win the fifth game, and there is a glimmer of hope.

That hope begins to build during the first half of Game 6 in Washington. Doug Collins is on fire and the Sixers look like they might forge a standoff and force a seventh game. But Unseld tips in an offensive rebound with less than 10 seconds to play and the Bullets go up by two points. Billy calls time and sets up a final play, hoping to force overtime. The plan is for Lloyd Free to utilize his considerable one-on-one talents, penetrate the Bullets' perimeter defense, and then dish off to Julius Erving. Game films later reveal Doc is there, and wide open. But Lloyd tries to force the action, throws an elbow into Elvin Hayes, and is called for an offensive foul. The Sixers lose possession of the ball and expire, without ever getting off a shot.

It is another numbing playoff defeat, one more galling gulp from what seems like a bottomless cup of frustration. And there is a long drive home, which is made even longer by the knowledge of the kind of reception that waits: We Owe You *Two*.

There is also the sense that this team, in its present form, for all of its success, for all of its 105 victories the last two seasons, will exist no more. Something drastic will have to be done.

A week later, with the funeral past and the mourning giving way to yet another rebuilding challenge, Billy comes in and offers a different chorus to an old, familiar tune: "We've got to get George

McGinnis out of here."

Actually, George had recovered a bit. He had had a very productive regular season, although he had once again floundered in the playoffs. The team had won 55 games and had exceeded its home attendance record set the year before. Playing the role of devil's advocate, I argued that we had no assurance that coming up with a new team might not be a worse team. Billy's answer was that the regular season was nice, but it was merely a prelude, and in the NBA the playoffs were everything. And this team, in its present form, was never going to last through the playoffs.

It would always find a shadow to trip over.

It was ironic. We had spent so much time and effort in getting George to come to Philadelphia, and now we were spending as much time trying to move him out. This time around, however, the other teams in the league seemed more receptive.

Billy's feeling was that while the Sixers were a running team, which was the style he favored, they didn't really have a guard to run the break, to orchestrate the tempo. Doug and Lloyd and Henry Bibby were "off" guards, primarily shooters.

The most visible player in the collegiate draft that spring of 1978 was Phil Ford, who had set all sorts of assists records at North Carolina during a four-year career. Billy, having played at Carolina, was tight with Coach Dean Smith. The problem was that the first pick in that draft belonged to Indiana. So we tried to make a deal with them, in which George McGinnis would return to his native state and his old team. In fact, we did make a deal, George for their draft pick, with us picking up part of George's $400,000 a year contract. There was the added proviso that we had to take back Melvin Bennett, whom we had traded to them earlier. He still had three years' guaranteed salary and Indiana was strapped financially and wanted to get his salary off its payroll.

The last remaining obstacle was George McGinnis himself because he had a no-trade clause in his contract with the Sixers. It gave him the right to refuse or approve any trade we might generate.

So on a bright spring day, Billy and I drove out to see George at his mansion in Villanova on the Main Line. It was a gorgeous house and we settled down around a table next to his swimming pool. George was low-key, cordial, but noncommital. He wanted time to think about it, he said. We gave the Pacers permission to talk with George, and he said he wanted an extension of his current contract. Indiana replied that they would need some sort of financial relief in that event. We were so desperate to make the deal that we even agreed to that. We would pick up some of George's contract. It was going to cost us in the neighborhood of $1.1 million, which is a pretty expensive neighborhood.

Fitz Dixon refused. You couldn't blame him. The deal made no good business sense at all. So, one week before the draft, the deal collapses.

The only salvation was that Indiana had indicated they were not interested in Phil Ford, so the Sixers didn't have to worry about losing him in the first selection of the draft. That meant we had to try to secure the second pick, which belonged to Kansas City. We negotiated with them and put together all sorts of packages. One player they insisted be part of the package was Joe Bryant. But he had had a brilliant playoff against the Bullets, had been one of the few Sixers' bright spots. We balked at getting rid of him and offered a counter proposal. The morning before the draft, KC turned us down.

And then, that night, when everyone had gone home and the switchboard was closed down, the light on my private phone line lit up. It was Carl Scheer, the Denver GM, and immediately he's trying to talk me into taking Bobby Jones. Denver will take George McGinnis off our hands, he says.

But they also insist we take Ralph Simpson, a player who isn't helping them and who has two guaranteed years left, at over $200,000 a year. Carl and I negotiated right into the early morning. We agreed, although it really grieved me to give up our own No. 1 pick, which Carl demanded. I told Carl: "We'll do this, but we also need a first-round draft pick from you. Let's make it a first rounder in any draft between 1980 and 1984, and you can choose the year." He agreed. "It'll be in '84."

So now we were unloading George at last and we were getting Bobby Jones, a big, fast, intelligent player with an ideal temperament. The quintessential team player. Most importantly, a player who was very coachable. That was certainly going to be something new on the Sixers. And a volatile offensive team was also going to get the game's best defensive forward. Bobby Jones would come to be known in Philly as The White Shadow.

But the Sixers' most pressing need was still a running guard, a whip-cracker on the fast break.

The answer would be supplied that very day, in the draft, in the second round. The 36th pick overall of the 1978 draft, taken by the Sixers, was Maurice Edward Cheeks, out of West Texas State.

For that, we can thank Jack McMahon, the ruddy old Brooklyn Irishman, the St. John's ace who went on to play in the NBA as a play-making guard himself, the feeder of Cliff Hagan and Bob Pettit on the old St. Louis Hawks, Oscar Robertson's coach at Cincinnati and a few other ABA stops.

It was Jack who had first seen Cheeks. That was back in November of '77. The Sixers were in New Orleans for a game and Jack swung over to West Texas State on another of his endless talent sorties, and he saw a very mediocre team which played a deliberate half-court game. But Jack's marvelous sense for the game saw something else. His intuition told him that Cheeks could play firewagon basketball even though he was trapped on a slow-down team. Other scouts saw Cheeks but they didn't see what Jack saw, which is just one more tribute to his instincts and his ability to make an evaluation. We arranged, after the collegiate season ended, for Cheeks to be brought to Cincinnati by an attorney there, Ron Grinker, to work out privately for us. There were a dozen players on the court and Maurice showed flashes of promise. He was quiet, introverted, just as he is today.

Prior to this, in the Pizza Hut Classic, a post-season game for collegiate seniors, Maurice was devastating. He completely dominated Butch Lee, the All-American from Marquette and a highly publicized player, and we cringed. We were afraid our cover had been blown in that game. Maurice Cheeks was no longer a secret. Yet somehow he was still there when it was the Sixers' turn to draft in the second round in the summer of '78, even though some NBA teams had had three picks by then.

The Sixers, happily, had Maurice Cheeks. Plus the rights to Bobby Jones.

But both George McGinnis and Bobby Jones had no-trade clauses. For two solid months I negotiated with their agents, the longest such bargaining in history. In mid-August each agreed to waive his no-trade, and it was hello Bobby, goodbye George.

The welcoming of The White Shadow was exciting. The leaving of George was poignant. For all of his shortcomings and his playoff collapses, we still owed George McGinnis a debt. He had resurrected a dead franchise in Philadelphia. And he and his wife, Lynda, had come to love Philly. They truly did not want to leave. He had been so reluctant to come here in the first place, and now we practically had to use dynamite to get him out of town.

I've always thought that, deep down, George's problem was that he really didn't enjoy basketball all that much. He had gotten by on his agility and strength and God-given skills, but he wouldn't work to correct his weaknesses, and over the summer he hardly touched a basketball. He was just not immersed, absorbed, in the game. It was an attitude the Sixers could not afford any longer. So George left, and it was a sad ending to what could have been a beautiful story.

Four years later the Telex in the Sixers' office would clatter out George's professional obituary: Indiana had released him; he was available to anyone. There were no takers.

As for the Sixers, training camp was about to open for the 1978–79 season, and the work now centered around trying to erase the memories of We Owe You One. . . .

6

Can't Anybody Here Play Guard?

THE 76ERS WERE like a snazzy sports car, all sleek and streamlined, chrome and glitter, neon flash and sequin splash. A truly classy chassis. But there was increasing concern about what kind of engine was under that gaudy hood. Sports cars are great for acceleration. But an NBA season is more marathon than sprint, and in the play-offs, especially, *var-o-o-o-o-m* becomes less important than stamina. You need a team that will last, that will endure through adversity, not an expensive showroom model that tends to self-destruct and spray parts all over the landscape.

In the summer of 1978, Billy Cunningham and his coaching aides, Jack McMahon and Chuck Daly, confirmed what they had suspected before—that, as exciting as this team was, it could not hold up, could not win a title. So it had to be re-tooled.

The Sixers had subtracted George McGinnis and had added Bobby Jones. The coaches felt Philly had gotten the better of that equation by far. Bobby Jones was a sacrificial, hard-working kind of player, the polar opposite of George, and would pair up at forward with Julius Erving much more favorably in style and temperament.

Bobby was neither child prodigy nor gifted athlete. He was gawky and awkward growing up, one of those kids who woke up each day and discovered, to his considerable chagrin, that there was more of him than there had been the night before, and he wasn't quite sure what to do with all those outsized feet, long legs and bony arms. He was the classic late bloomer, blossoming not in high school but later on in college, at North Carolina.

He was built like Ichabod Crane, and to this day still looks gaunt and stringy, with a chest that is almost sunken, eyes buried deep inside hollow sockets, walking with a jangly, loose-limbed, slope-shouldered sort of gait. This storklike appearance masks, however, the soaring spirit of an eagle. Opponents long ago learned to disregard Bobby's deceptive mien because he can explode to the basket, cheeks puffing in concentration, eyes blazing, elbows hacking a path to the hoop.

It is quite possible that if Bobby Jones had been born with the physical attributes of, say, a George McGinnis, he might never have developed into an All-Star. But because he started with more limitations than assets, he made himself into a great player. For one thing, in the beginning, he wanted no part of offense. Normally, that's what kids live for, a chance to shoot the ball. But Bobby felt so uncoordinated that he shunned the ball, concentrated instead on defense, which is the ditch-digging aspect of the game, the drudgery.

He had been pushed into the sport by his father. He was a pale, gaunt kid in junior high and his father tired of seeing him sprawled in front of the TV set, getting paler and gaunter. At Chapel Hill, under the tutelage of Dean Smith, he became a complete, all-around player, a defensive terror, exceptional passer, and a considerable offensive threat because he shot as accurately with his left hand as he did with his right.

Oh, yes, there was one thing more. Some people choose to regard it as a handicap; Bobby Jones is not among them. It is called epilepsy, and for a long time it was the disease society whispered about, distastefully trading images of convulsions, spasms, frothing, seizures. Bobby Jones is an epileptic, yet he plays professionl basketball for a living, and that is made possible by constant monitoring, medication, and his own indomitable spirit.

"I've been telling people for years he's got to be the top candidate for most courageous athlete of the year," says Al Domenico, the Sixers' longtime trainer. "No one can do what he does. He goes out there game after game with the possibility he could have a seizure in front of all America. It takes a man of a special breed to do what he does."

He has done public TV commercials for the Epilepsy Foundation.

"It's such a misunderstood disease," he said. "I've only had a few seizures, and then when they're over, for me it's been like taking a nap. I wake up, it's all over. It's my wife or whoever is around that faces the real ordeal. She knows to take something, like my wallet, and stuff it in my mouth so I don't choke or swallow my tongue. Once, she tried to use her hand and I almost bit off her finger. Anyway, I take my medication, get my rest, take care of myself, and really I haven't had that many problems. The theme of those commercials we did was that epilepsy is not what you think, and even with it you *can* be successful."

His wife, Tess, whom he met in college, reawakened his commitment to Jesus Christ, and one of the first things he did when he joined the Sixers was come to me about starting a chapel before Sunday afternoon games, a practice that had grown and spread throughout baseball and football. I still remember that first chapel session, in February. Our speaker was Melvin Floyd, a black inner-city youth worker. Three players showed up—Bobby, Doc, and Kent Benson, who was then with Milwaukee. Now all the teams in the NBA have chapels, and that's been a spinoff of Bobby's efforts.

Anyway, when training camp opened in 1978, we knew we were getting the quintessential team player in The White Shadow, and he represented the first step in a new effort to mold the kind of team Billy wanted. Bobby Jones plays the game with the same sort of intensity that Billy had.

What Billy also wanted was a running team, one that would

scorch other teams, hit them with a 20-2 spurt and never look back. The Sixers, however, had lacked a true point guard, and were hoping that the other new face in camp, the rookie from West Texas State, would help furnish part of the answer.

Camp had been moved from Ursinus College because Billy felt the Tartan surface there was too hard on the players' legs, did not have enough give. He wanted a wooden floor, so the Sixers had moved pre-season training to Franklin and Marshall College in Lancaster, Pennsylvania. And from the very first day, the new kid looked in charge. Maurice Cheeks never did appear to be a rookie. He stepped right in and began running the break, igniting the set offense, setting exactly the sort of tempo Billy wanted. Maurice became a starter, which was a significant feat considering the talent on that team.

Rarely do first-year players win a starting spot, and those who do usually are No. 1 draft picks with megabucks contracts and "can't-miss" stamped all over them. But here was this quiet, shy kid from a mediocre college team hardly anyone had heard of and he not only blended right in, he took command. Strictly by his play, however. Mo's voice never was raised and even today it remains hushed. He plays the game with his face furrowed in concentration, creased by something between a frown and a scowl, the ever-present wad of chewing gum sticking sideways out of a corner of his mouth, as though he is signaling for a right-hand turn.

Mo Cheek's style of play has always been like his temperament: low-key, economical, bare-bones fundamental. There are no frills, no flair for the theatrical. He plays a position that is the most visible on the floor because the point guard either has the ball or he is distributing it, and yet Mo shuns the spotlight. You never see him throw passes between his legs or behind his back, none of that French pastry. His passes tend to be basic, two-handed, but they get there and result in two points; there is, after all, no bonus for showmanship. Too, he has the hands of a pickpocket, and ever since he has been in the league he has been among the leaders in assists and steals. He is as good as anyone in the league at pushing the ball up the court, and he has come to master all the subtleties of his position, knowing which player wants the ball at a particular moment in the game, where he prefers to receive it, and how.

Mo would just as soon play the game, dress and leave. Remember that the team he was joining was a nightly media event, one that was brashly talkative and led the NBA in nicknames, hyperbole and self-advertisement. Even now, Mo is barely visible in the locker room, submitting to interviews but plainly relieved when they are over. About all the press has been able to pry out of Mo Cheeks' private life is that he loves dogs and chocolate chip cookies. And, of course, basketball.

As it became clear that the rookie was ideally suited to run the team, Billy was, at the same time, becoming increasingly uncomfortable with Lloyd Free. Lloyd was not a role player. He was a stunning offensive talent, but he was also the kind of player who had to have the ball in his hands, and once it was there it was rarely going anywhere else except in the direction of the basket.

"Lloyd is just never going to fit in here with the kind of team we're trying to build," said Billy. "How about seeing what you can get for him?"

So we shopped him around but no other team showed any interest. We knew why. It was Lloyd's style of play. He had to have center stage, and when he was in the game the whole style and pace of play changed. The flow was interrupted. Lloyd had the ball and the other four players ended up standing around and watching, wondering what he was going to try next, and as a result they were not maneuvering themselves into rebounding position, or working to get free themselves, and frequently were caught in too deep and beaten down the floor in the transition game. Lloyd Free was a great individual talent, and he still is. Few people seriously argued when he legally changed his name to World B. Free. But the price you had to pay in terms of team success was simply too high. Lloyd was a luxury no one could afford.

He was plagued by personal problems at that time as well, his finances in total disarray, and that carried over onto the court. His concentration was fragmented. About all he had going for him was a long-term contract. But Billy was determined to reshape this team, surround himself with more coachable players, ones less concerned with individual statistics, and he had decided that with Mo Cheeks' rapid start, plus Doug Collins, Henry Bibby and the newly acquired Ralph Simpson, those four would comprise the guard line. Lloyd Free didn't have much of a future in Philadelphia.

Finally, literally in the last hour before the final roster cutdown before the start of the '78-'79 season, San Diego called. They faced an enormous rebuilding job and they needed some guaranteed points in their starting lineup, someone they could count on for points every night. The new coach in San Diego was none other than Gene Shue, the old master of reclamation and salvage. He said he would take a chance with Lloyd. So, five minutes before the cutdown deadline, we struck a deal—Lloyd Free for a first-round draft pick. And who would that be? He remains a mystery player. In return for Free, the Sixers got San Diego's first round draft in 1984. The Sixers were in such a bind and so desperate to get rid of Lloyd that we even agreed to pick up a portion of his salary for that year; it amounted to around $25,000.

Lloyd hopped a plane to Phoenix, where San Diego was to open the season, and proceeded to score 21 points. He has, of course, been among the NBA's scoring leaders ever since, but then there never was any doubt about his ability to put the ball in the hole.

So the Sixers began the 1978-79 season, against a background chorus of We Owe You *Two*, as a strengthened team, rid of Lloyd Free and George McGinnis, and fortified with Bobby Jones and Mo Cheeks. But the team had also lost some of its charisma in the eyes of the fans, who missed the carnival atmosphere, and that was reflected at the gate. Attendance began to slip, which seemed to be in direct violation of the commonly accepted practice that fans will always support a winner. Well, this new team that was being forged merely won its first nine games of the new season, playing precisely the kind of ball Billy wanted.

It seemed too good to be true. And, of course, it was.

In January, Doug Collins' foot gives way and collapses, a stress fracture in the ankle area. Since the foot surgery that had pretty much wiped out his rookie season, Doug had put together a stretch of relatively healthy, injury-free seasons, developing into one of the game's premier players. He was relentless on the court, throwing himself into every game, playing every minute as though it were the very last thing he would ever do. A bad game would nearly reduce him to tears and he would brood about it, chafing for the next game and a chance at redemption. He was very emotional, a highly charged sort; he was also insecure, needing constant reassurance. Doctors later commented that his arch structure was definitely not designed for basketball, especially the way he played it. He was a non-stop frenzy, running with such force and explosion that he would literally rip the soles out of his sneakers. In high school, Doug had once recalled, his coach would send him out running and would follow behind him in a battered old car, and whenever Doug began to lag while struggling up a hill, he would feel the prodding nudge of that car's fenders against his legs. He always did play as if an invisible car was gaining on him. But all of that jarring stop-start, those abrupt cuts and changes of direction, that sneaker-squealing music of the game, was eroding his feet.

The stress fracture was hard to spot, even in the X-rays. There was some conjecture about how serious the injury really was. Doug's first operation had been performed by Dr. Joseph Torg, who had been the Sixers' team physician, and Doug would deal with no other doctor. Since Dr. Torg was no longer the team physician, that meant some problems. Surgery was required again this time. Doug returned in time to play again in March, and did well for a short stretch, but then the foot blew out again and he was grounded.

Unwittingly, I made a comment, for publication, that Doug happened to have a low threshold of pain. I didn't mean that in a derogatory sense at all, but Doug took it personally, as though it were a direct slap in his face, a questioning of his courage or his desire. Anyone who had ever seen him play would never question that. I apologized to him, but it was a long time before he got over it.

The bulk of that season became a frantic repair job, the Sixers trying to patch up their guard line.

Ralph Simpson was clearly not the great player he had been in the ABA, and Billy soon lost confidence in him. With Doug out, that left the Sixers with the rookie, Cheeks, and with Henry Bibby, who was reliable if unspectacular on offense but who was also small, and that presented defensive problems because other teams would take advantage of his size and post him up at every opportunity.

We were scouring the waiver wire, trying to hunt up a guard. The only real "extra" player we had at the time was Harvey Catchings. He was the No. 3 center, playing behind Darryl Dawkins and Caldwell Jones, which meant he was hardly playing at all. The only team with a surplus of guards was the New Jersey Nets. That season, they were a real hodge-podge of characters, a collection of hot dogs and renegades. They offered us one of their starting guards, either John Williamson or Eric Money. We debated and finally settled on Money, and we also took from them another guard, Al Skinner, who had been a college teammate of Julius Erving at the University of Massachusetts. But we also used the same strong-arm tactics on them which Denver had used on us. We told them we'd take Money and Skinner and give them Catchings, but they also had to take Ralph Simpson from us, along with most of his guaranteed contract.

They agreed.

It would turn out that we were still applying band-aids when some serious surgery was required. The Sixers would spend the better part of two years trying to shore up the guard line.

Eric Money was a talented little player. There were streaks when he looked like a miniature Oscar Robertson, and probably we had been influenced to take him because he had had some big games against us. But, like Lloyd Free, his talent was partially offset by personal problems. He was alleged to be involved in a number of paternity suits, there were rumors of drugs, and he had a reputation around the league as surly and uncoachable. It must be emphasized, however, that in his time with us he never presented a problem.

Except that out on the court, because he wasn't tall and couldn't handle defensive pressure, we were shackled with a guard line that simply didn't match up well against almost every other team.

The Sixers made a creditable enough showing that season, finishing with 47 wins and 35 losses. That was 12 games over .500. It was also, incidentally, the *worst* year the Sixers have ever had with Billy Cunningham as coach.

The team finished second in their division, seven games behind Washington, which was defending its world championship.

In the miniseries to open the playoffs, the Sixers faced New Jersey and won comfortably, the first game by eight points, the second by ten.

Then it's on to the semifinals and the opponent is San Antonio, with George Gervin and Larry (Special K) Kenon. The Ice Man Cometh, and he brings the Spurs with him. Ice Gervin is one of those players who do things so effortlessly it makes you cry. The Sixers get all of one day's respite from the Nets series and trek on down to San Antonio, where they promptly lose two games. They win only one in the Spectrum and head back to Texas, down 3-1, and this looks like a carbon copy of the previous spring's debacle against the Bullets.

But in an amazing performance, certainly one nobody expected, the Sixers trample the Spurs in the shadow of the Alamo, come back home and win in Philly, and suddenly it's 3-3 and it's the Spurs who feel the noose tightening around their necks. To this point, the Spurs were saddled with their own playoff stigma. They had never won a playoff series, and now here they were, having blown a 3-1 lead.

The Sixers are still woefully shorthanded at guard, to the point of even swinging Doc to the back court. But there is hardly any outside scoring threat at all, and so the Spurs, like every other opponent that year, can sag back, pack in their defense around the basket, which gives them a big rebounding edge.

That seventh game is a cauldron of noise and pressure. The Spurs are urged on by a howling band of beery zealots who call themselves the Baseline Bums. They are the verbal equivalent of green chili burritos. They are great to have on your side, but when you are playing against their beloved Spurs, you get a new appreciation for the word "intimidation."

In the first minute of that decisive game, Darryl Dawkins sprains his ankle and limps to the dressing room. He tries to come back, but the ankle won't hold up. The Sixers are down to circle-the-wagons time. Despite their depleted roster, they somehow manage to have the lead going into the final two and a half minutes. But they cannot hold it. The unfathomable part is that the Spurs' heroics are supplied not by the Ice Man nor by Special K, the two you would logically expect, but by Mike Green, Allan Bristow, Louie Dampier and Coby Dietrick. Let's just say that none of them was a threat to make the All-Star team that year. Or any other.

San Antonio wins, 111-108.

The Sixers have been bounced from the playoffs once more.

I remember trying to run out the frustration afterwards. I went out for a midnight jog, probably subconsciously hoping to be mugged. All of San Antonio was a cacophony of horns and sirens; it was Mardi Gras in San Antonio.

Now we owed two for sure, and we would not be allowed to forget that.

So we went into the summer of 1979 sifting through ashes once again, and the most pressing concern was still the guard line. The one bit of redemption had been Mo Cheeks. He had delivered during the regular season, but there is always concern about how a rookie will respond in the playoffs. All Mo had done was average 18.8 points a game and shoot 54 percent.

But beyond Mo and Henry Bibby were only question marks. No one knew whether Doug Collins could come back from that foot injury. Eric Money and Al Skinner were stop-gap measures; they weren't going to take us anywhere. So the Sixers' obvious point of emphasis in the upcoming draft would have to be big guards.

Just before the draft came word of a Baker League phenom named Billy Ray Bates. He had played at Kentucky State, was drafted by Houston, then cut by them. He had drifted up to Maine, in the Continental Basketball Association. He had the build of a thoroughbred; he was fast and springy. Jack McMahon watched him play in the Baker League and came back and said: "He's the best guard I've seen all year." We brought him in for a private workout and signed him to a two-year contract, with the first year guaranteed at $60,000. That looked like a running start on our biggest problem. It would later turn out to be more of a lurch and a stumble than a running start . . . .

In the first round of the draft, the Sixers take Jim Spanarkel of Duke, 6-5, good passer, team player, smart, coachable; appears to have a lot of Bobby Jones' traits. Unfortunately, it will turn out he does not have Bobby's speed nor first step.

In the second round, the Sixers take Clint Richardson, 6-3, long arms, quick jumper, who had actually played forward at the University of Seattle. But we had brought him in for a private workout, too, and felt he could be converted to guard. His brother had played professional football and his sister was a talented track and field competitor. Clint was a soft-spoken, sincere kid, the kind of coachable player Billy liked.

So there were Bates and Spanarkel and Richardson, and the Sixers were prepared to go to training camp once more, to get ready for the 1979-80 season, convinced that they had plugged all those gaping holes in their guard line. They would find, in fact, that it would require almost another whole year to complete the patching. Those plugs had a distressing habit of springing new leaks . . . .

7

Magic

MURPHY'S LAW: If anything can go wrong, it will.

MURPHY'S FIRST COROLLARY: Nothing is as easy as it looks.

MURPHY'S SECOND COROLLARY: Everything takes longer than you think.

MURPHY'S THIRD COROLLARY: If there is a possibility of several things going wrong, the one that will cause the most damage will be the one to go wrong.

Murphy, obviously, has been a longtime holder of 76ers' season tickets.

The Sixers open training camp for the 1979-80 season still trying to answer the burning question from the last season: Can't anybody here play guard? Maurice Cheeks, in his rookie year, had demonstrated, rather emphatically, that he could. But depth was the problem, and it was rather desperately hoped that some salvation could be found from the three newcomers—the spectacularly skilled Billy Ray Bates, and the two big draft choices, Jim Spanarkel and Clint Richardson.

In all of those drills that require only raw athletic skills, Billy Ray Bates excels. He wins the mile run, he wins every wind sprint. His talent in undeniable. The problem arises when he must harness that talent and mesh it within a team concept. As set plays are installed, Billy Ray becomes confused. He is unable to retain much of anything. And when he is put in a position of having to think, he becomes hesitant and there is a corresponding drop-off in his skills. It will be discovered later what had been suspected; he is an illiterate. By the pre-season, he is tied in knots of frustration, and the Sixers waive him. He will drift back to Maine and play minor league ball, but Steve Kauffman, a hard-working Philadelphia attorney, will land him with Portland, and Billy Ray will help them into the playoffs and then have two more productive seasons for the Trail Blazers. He will become immensely popular with the fans there. But he will remain an unsophisticated farm boy from Mississippi who simply is not ready for life in the fast lane. He will succumb to the lure of drugs and alcohol, and be in and out of rehabilitation centers. At last report he will drift off to Manila to try pro ball in the Philippines.

That leaves the Sixers with the draft choices. It is known that Spanarkel lacks speed, but it becomes clear in camp how distressingly lacking he is. He can't get off a shot; virtually every attempt is blocked. He will spend the season on the bench, and later go to Dallas in the expansion draft, where he will manage to hang on, providing the Mavericks with some offense in their formative years.

As for Clint Richardson, it looks as if he, too, will not pan out. The conversion from forward to guard is difficult and he struggles. As the exhibition season progresses, Clint seems to retrogress. The Sixers, in fact, are ready to release him. And then, in Pittsburgh, in a pre-season game with the New Orleans Jazz, he gives a brilliant performance. I actually had his plane ticket back to Seattle in my coat pocket and was going to give it to him that very night. But he earned a last-minute reprieve with his effort that evening. I doubt if Clint knew how close he was to being exiled then. It would turn out, of course, to be the wisest non-move possible. He has been a solid contributor ever since.

Clint's resurgence enables the Sixers to release Eric Money. He had been a model citizen with the Sixers but for some reason did not play well, and was let go two weeks into the season.

Doug Collins, meanwhile, had done another Lazarus job, came back from surgery and was playing with his usual verve and abandon. So the Sixers open the year with Mo and Doug starting at guard, Henry Bibby, Clint and Spanarkel backing them up.

Just before the season starts, the Sixers make one more roster cut. Joe Bryant. He had not played all that much the year before and he had complained, openly, bitterly, about it. He probably sealed his doom in a playoff game with San Antonio when he finally got in, and almost immediately launched a 30-foot bomb while practically falling out of bounds. It looked as if it had been done purely out of spite. Billy Cunningham couldn't get him out of the game fast enough. JB wasn't going to have much of a future with the Sixers, so we began to shop him around. We found a receptive ear in San Diego, where Gene Shue was preparing for his second season as coach. We were particularly anxious to bail out on JB because he had won a contract extension earlier, after his big contributions against Washington in the playoffs of '78. We were able to extract from San Diego a first-round draft pick. But it was way, way down the road. In 1986 to be precise. I remember joking at the time that somewhere floating around in America was a 15-year-old phenom who will be just ripe when that pick comes around.

So the 1979-80 season starts, and it's a good one. Doug Collins is playing well. The Sixers will have a glorious year, winning 59 games, losing but 23. Normally, you lap the rest of the field with a record like that. Except Boston was even hotter. They had been floundering badly the last couple of years, but that previous summer they had drafted Larry Bird, and rarely has a rookie had such an immediate impact. His presence completely turned the Celtics around. The year before, they had been 29-53. With Bird, they were 61-21, and finished two games ahead of the Sixers.

Early in this season, there occurred two games that would become memorable and receive international attention. The focal point of each was Darryl Dawkins.

105

On November 5, 1979, in a game at Kansas City, Darryl had the ball and came crashing in from the right side, soaring up for a dunk. The only Kansas City defender near the basket was Bill Robinzine and his momma hadn't raised a fool; Robinzine wasn't about to contest Darryl in full flight. So he just stood there, spectating. The next thing he knew, he was taking a shower . . . a shower of plexiglass. For Darryl, while slamming the ball through the net, had smashed the rim with his forearms with such violent force that the backboard simply exploded, the glass shattering and raining down in a million pieces. It was an awesome sight. Robinzine reflexively covered his head and scurried for safety. Shards and splinters of glass ricocheted all over the building. It took the better part of an hour to mop up and replace the backboard.

Darryl, of course, became an instant celebrity. Every TV station in America ran a tape of Dawkins' destruction, this young Colossus, Sampson-like, bringing down structures in a shower of ruin. Darryl, innately glib anyway, by now had perfected jive-talk and a smooth disc-jockey kind of patter. He was very much into rhyme and hyperbole, and had taken to anointing himself with neon nicknames. He had amazing spring for a man-child of 6-10 and 260 pounds, and his specialty was the dunk. He had a wide-ranging variety, and he lovingly named each one. There were, in his arsenal of dunks, the following: Yo Moma, In Your Face Disgrace, Cover Yo Damn Head, Left-Handed Spine Chiller Supreme, Sexophonic Turbo Delight, Earthquake Breaker, Hammer of Thor, and, finally, the No-Playin'-Get-Out-Of-The-Wayin'-Backboard-Swayin'-Game-Delayin' Super Spike. Darryl had no peer at talking trash and he obligingly filled writers' notebooks with tales from his rich imagination. He claimed two mysterious planets as his residence—Lovetron and Chocolate Paradise. He said he specialized in interplanetary funkmanship, though it was never made clear what exactly that was. He needed five minutes after each game just to get his jewelry on, gold and diamond doo-dads, including several strings of necklaces, each emblazoned with several of his personally conceived nicknames, among them Sir Slam, Dr. Dunk, Chocolate Thunder and Master of Disaster.

106

But this latest feat, this shattering of a backboard, taxed even the poet in his soul. He sensed immediately the impact his Kansas City detonation would have, and after a night of courting the muse, grandly announced that henceforward what we had witnessed in KC would be forever known as this kind of dunk: "Chocolate Thunder flyin', Robinzine cryin', teeth-shaking, glass-breaking, rump-roastin', bun-toastin', wham, bam, glass!"

Say that fast 10 times.

Darryl fairly oozed charisma and there was an appealing charm about him. He was not malicious and he was obviously having so much fun out of living that you could not take offense at his wild braggadocio. It was just that Darryl never did develop into what we thought he had the potential to be. Although he was capable of some incandescent moves and thunder dunks, he was never able to sustain them over any significant period. But he was undeniably one certified box office attraction.

While the rest of the country was talking excitedly about the backboard shattering, the league office indicated to the Sixers that it took a dim view of such events. Rather curtly, the Commissioner informed us: "That is not to happen again."

Three weeks later, it did.

This was against San Antonio, in the Spectrum. Up goes Darryl, down comes another backboard, the glass first taking on the appearance of a mammoth spider web and then exploding in another shower. There was a giant gasp from the crowd. The promoter in me went running onto the floor with a paper bag, scooping up the slivers. We announced that for the following Sunday's game, the giveaway attraction would be pieces of that glass, sort of like handing out chunks of solidified lava from the eruption of Mount Vesuvius.

That promotion died stillborn, however. Billy, Darryl and I were tersely summoned to the Commissioner's office for a 2 P.M. meeting the next day. We walked down Fifth Avenue and it was almost a ticker tape parade, heads turning, fingers pointing, people calling out to Darryl. He had become Paul Bunyan in sneakers. The man on the street clearly loved what Darryl had done. The Commissioner didn't. Darryl said the shattered backboards had been "accidents." Larry O'Brien sternly ordered him to avoid any further "accidents." He spent almost as much time scolding me, and said there definitely would be no glass giveaway in Philadelphia. From that meeting, there emerged what would become known as the Dawkins Rule: any player who shattered a backboard would be automatically ejected, fined, and made ineligible to play the following game. It was also from that the experimentation began with snap-back rims, which have since come into wide usage. They lessen the vulnerability of the backboards.

Darryl Dawkins was, and is, a real physical specimen. The consensus is that he is the strongest basketball player this side of Wilt Chamberlain. But the pity is that Darryl never really knew how to use his gifts. He has an uncanny shooting touch from outside for a man his size, and he is so enamored of it that all through his career in Philly he would launch those long-range jumpshots instead of powering to the basket. It was almost as though he were afraid to use his great strength, afraid to "put it all on the line."

But during that season Darryl became a genuine curiosity piece. As I made the banquet circuit rounds, the people couldn't get enough Darryl Dawkins stories. They were fascinated by this monolith. I told so many tales I even began to believe some of them myself, including the questionnaire (fictional, of course) which we had asked Darryl to fill out. It contained such questions and answers as:

Q: When were you born, Darryl?
A: January 11th, 12th, and 13th.
Q: Your church preference?
A: Red brick.
Q: And what is your race?
A: The mile.
Q: What's your alma mater?
A: Always do your best.

108

Q: What's your best position?
A: Crouched over a little, like this.
Q: What's your sign?
A: Slippery when wet.
Q: If you could be reincarnated, what would you like to come back as?
A: As soon as possible.

The Sixers are locked in a duel with Boston, and the guard line seems to be holding up, but at about the midway point of the season Doug Collins begins to develop the same sort of symptoms of the previous season. By late January, his other foot blows out. More surgery, more casts, more crisis on the guard line.

Clint Richardson becomes a starter despite his youth and inexperience, and he will do a reasonably good job as a rookie. Still, help is needed. The Sixers put out an all-points bulletin for a guard. Again.

Several are available, but one name that is especially intriguing surfaces. Pete Maravich. The White Globetrotter. Once he could make a basketball sit up and talk. Now he was well into the twilight of his playing career. He was off knee surgery, which made his future—at his age, particularly—suspect. He was mired on the Utah Jazz bench. But his name alone was still box office, and the Sixers' attendance had been declining for the last two years. Billy was intrigued; was there half a year of good basketball left in Maravich?

The Jazz waived him and we flew him in for a medical examination and for interviews. Ironically, my last act as the GM in Atlanta in 1974 had been to trade Pete to New Orleans—for four first-round draft picks plus a couple of players. Pete never got over that, and his bitterness toward me had been evident for years. Now I met him at the airport and we both laughed, in amazement, at how things were working out. He had dinner with Billy. The Sixers' attitude was one of caution; this was strictly exploratory work. But Pete's presence in Philadelphia was ferreted out by the media and they wrote the story as though the deal had already been arranged. There was no doubt; Pete was coming to the Sixers. In fact, while we were sorely tempted, we still weren't completely sure we wanted him. We also didn't know that he had arranged a similar visit to Boston. Only at the end of our conversation did he tell us he was calling on the Celtics. Well, he decided to sign with Boston. What he had done, simply, was take a calculated gamble between the two teams, opting to go with the one he felt had the best chance to reach the finals of the playoffs.

It would turn out that he guessed wrong.

So Pete Maravich is a Celtic now. Billy didn't seem all that disturbed. But the Sixers' owner was. Fitz Dixon's reaction was one of stunned disbelief. He had read all the reports in the papers and assumed that the Sixers had Maravich locked up, and now Maravich had suddenly gotten away. Worse, he had been pirated from under our noses by the very team we were chasing. We came off looking as if we had bungled things, and Fitz's response was: Okay, who bungled this?

As late January, 1980, arrived, the Maravich escapade was still rankling Fitz, but no one realized it would become a trigger point for upheaval within the organization.

On January 30, around noon, I got a call from Ralph Bernstein, the long-time sports editor of the Associated Press in Philadelphia. He said: "We have a report that Lou Scheinfeld is about to be hired as the president of the 76ers. We'd like a comment from you."

My only comment was: "This is the first I've heard about it."

Two hours later, we were summoned to a meeting with Fitz and were informed that Scheinfeld, indeed, was in. Fitz said this would be a major marketing thrust on his part, that Scheinfeld's job would be to generate a greater ticket response. Attendance had been falling and Fitz was losing money with the Sixers. It would turn out, however, that this would be Fitz's last major act as owner.

Scheinfeld had been a young executive in the Flyers-Spectrum empire of Ed Snider. He had established his reputation as a promoter with a certain flair. He had dabbled with the Flyers, the

110

Spectrum, and with cable TV, but he had never stayed in any one job for very long. He had a harsh, abrasive manner which alienated many people. When he had been president of the Spectrum, he and I had been involved in negotiations for a long-term lease, and they had been far from pleasant. We were not exactly bosom buddies. He had laid the groundwork for the Spectrum's strangling lease with the Sixers. While it was very lucrative for the Spectrum, it has been a financial albatross around the Sixers' neck. It is the toughest lease in professional basketball.

By now, Fitz was well into his fourth year as owner of the Sixers. In many ways, I always suspected he had bought the team for his son, George, who had hopped around, and Fitz was hoping some day George would become deeply involved with the team. But it became apparent that George had no interest in the team. So the Sixers evolved into a two-headed operation directed by Hunter McMullin and myself, Hunter handling the office part and me the basketball end. We had, over a period, come to an agreement that we could function; we had an uneasy alliance, but it worked. But the hiring of Scheinfeld left Hunter with basically nothing to do, and, ironically, served to bring us closer together.

Lou Scheinfeld came in spending money with both hands. His approach was crisp, sharp, cold. He ran up enormous advertising bills, and then began firing people. The office was in constant turmoil. Lou had an unfortunate habit of speaking too quickly, of opening his mouth before he considered the implications. In an effort to be frank, he sometimes was far too blunt. As one example, we were trying at that time to get the Sixers' new mascot, Big Shot, off the ground. The town had fallen in love with one fuzzy, entertaining creature, the Phillie Phanatic, so competition was tough. Lou said, publicly, that Big Shot—our frizzy blue creation—was absurd. Worse, he stank. Well, I will admit that downwind he *did* tend to be a bit gamey, but to blatantly ridicule your own mascot, in public. . . . Within days, every personal appearance involving Big Shot had been canceled. Who wanted a "stinky" entertainer? So much for a major marketing thrust.

Also, Lou could be vitriolic about how the Spectrum was

111

operated. He said it was unsafe to go into that building during Sixers games. There were some security and sanitary problems to be worked out, but the Spectrum was hardly a muggers' clubhouse or a convention center for drug pushers as it became portrayed. Lou's unfortunate remarks in public set us back several years in terms of promotion and ticket-selling.

And then one Sunday afternoon, coming out of the Spectrum, Lou was asked a fairly innocuous question about Julius Erving's status, and he replied that he wanted Doc to have a lifetime contract with the 76ers, whatever that meant. Doc's agent, Irwin Weiner, immediately began salivating over that news. It was a chance remark, said without forethought, and it was an incredible *faux pas*, one that would ultimately cost the Sixers a ton of money. Ultimately, the Sixers did sign Doc to a longterm contract, in the fall of 1980. Lou, in desperation, had come to me and asked if we could get bailed out of the situation. We ended with a better deal than we had any right to expect, thanks, in part, to my long relationship with Doc and Irwin. They had been handed a loaded gun and they could have put it right to the Sixers' head if they had so desired. . . .

By now, it is early February of 1980 and the Sixers are still searching for guard help, and a new name suddenly pops up on the horizon: Lionel Hollins. He has a contract snag with Portland and an apparent run-in with Jack Ramsay over coaching philosophy. The Trail Blazers are in the process of dismantling the team that had beaten the Sixers for the world championship in 1977.

Billy wanted Lionel. That was understandable. Hollins was an experienced player, a defensive demon, and he functioned well within the team concept; he didn't have to have the ball to be effective; he was content to orchestrate, and he was proven under pressure. I called Stu Inman, the Portland GM, and the asking price was steep—they wanted our 1981 first-round draft pick which we had secured from Cleveland in the Terry Furlow deal. We had carefully stashed that pick away and guarded it. Cleveland was on its way to finishing deep in the standings, which meant that

112

was going to be a very early pick, making it even more valuable.

We cringed at the prospect of relinquishing it, but the bottom line was that the Sixers needed immediate help on the guard line. So we're about ready to agree, and then just before the trading deadline, Portland throws us a vicious curve. Inman calls and says: "My owner says we've also got to have $100,000. In cash."

I expected Fitz to give up at this point. But he's very competitive and he wanted a championship. So he said: "Spend it. Get him."

It wasn't quite that easy.

There was a clause in Hollins' contract giving him the right to approve any trade. He said that Philadelphia would be just fine with him. But . . . but he wanted a three-year extension of his contract, which would pay him over $350,000 a year. But we were cornered and everyone knew it. We agreed to that, too. Ultimately, of course, that large contract would lead to Lionel's trade to San Diego, as the Sixers frantically reduced their payroll in 1982 to accommodate the acquisition of Moses Malone.

Anyway, on February 8, 1980, Lionel (The Train) Hollins becomes a 76ers. He got in town on Saturday and the very next afternoon we played one of our big rivals, Los Angeles, at the Spectrum. Train played magnificently and the Sixers won. His impact was immediate, and his arrival solidified the team. Train and Mo started at guards, backed up by Henry Bibby and Clint Richardson. Billy was using his Twin Towers of Darryl Dawkins and Caldwell Jones up front, along with Doc, and had Bobby Jones and Steve Mix coming off the bench.

It was a good team, and it got even better because, miraculously, Doug Collins came back again. He had overcome his latest injury and was playing well. The guard line which had been such a source of vexation for a year and a half was now unexpectedly deep.

But in March, in a game against Washington, Doug twisted his knee. It just buckled. The team physician, Dr. Mike Clancy, took one look at it and shook his head. Once more, Dr. Torg had to cut into Doug Collins. It was Doug's third trip to the operating table in

113

two years. He was through for the season. Maybe for good. Through his travail, Doug had come to accept the Lord into his life. He felt his renewed faith would sustain him. It seemed as though he would get ample opportunity to find out now.

The Sixers' acquisition of Hollins now became even more crucial.

The team ends a great season, but Boston has an even greater one, and so the Sixers must play a miniseries. The opponent is Washington, and the Bullets are on the last legs of that brief dynasty that had won it all two years before. The Sixers wade right through them, in two straight, and continue on to the next round, against Atlanta, and the result is equally as impressive. The Hawks fall in five games.

Which sets up the confrontation everyone had been awaiting—Boston and Philly, winners of 121 games between them that season. Train is super. The Sixers get a split in Boston Garden, and then, stunningly, win the next three, including an 11-point triumph in the Garden in the fifth game.

After a big regular season, the Sixers have steam-rolled through the playoffs, winning 10 of 12 games, and simply trampling the favored Celtics. The debt is long overdue by now, but at last it looks like We Owe You One is going to be slam-dunked into the trash basket. The rebuilt team is on a roll now, and surely vengeance never will have tasted as sweet.

The 76ers are in the finals. Against the Los Angeles Lakers.

The series starts propitiously, with the Sixers earning a split out in LA. But they turn around and immediately dissipate that by losing one of the games in the Spectrum. Tied 2-2, the series shifts back across the country to the West Coast. In game 5, Kareem Abdul-Jabbar sprains his ankle early and limps off. Clearly, all the omens are favorable.

But then, right there in the shadow of Hollywood, Kareem drags himself back out, somehow, and plays in the fourth quarter. And, with the score tied, limping horribly, he somehow throws down a basket, is fouled, and sinks the free throw. That three-point play is the difference, and the Lakers win.

So now it's back to Philly, but Kareem's heroics have been costly. His ankle is so swollen, he is so incapacitated, that he doesn't even make the trip. He remains in LA, presumably to rest and be as ready as possible for the seventh game.

It is a game that will never be played.

The attitude of almost everyone coming into Game 6 at the Spectrum is one of "Why even bother with it?" The Lakers, by leaving Kareem at home to prepare for the next game, obviously have conceded this one. This one is considered nothing more than a walkover. It is a foregone conclusion. You can mail in the score. This is merely a formality.

It becomes, instead, a night of pure Magic.

Earvin (Magic) Johnson.

He should have been taking final exams at Michigan State. Instead, he stomped on the Sixers' fingers even as they were stretching for the final push up to the top of the mountain at last.

Magic played all five positions that night. He scored 42 points, snatched 15 rebounds, passed out 7 assists, made 3 steals. It was a virtuoso performance, an astonishing display of all-around ability. Magic put the torch to Philadelphia 123-107.

Once more, cruelly, the Sixers were a day late and a dollar short. One brick shy of a load.

The Lakers were the world champions. The Sixers had been done in by Magic.

It was probably just as well, but there was little time for the usual agonizing postmortems after this latest disaster. The draft was almost upon us, but even before that there was the matter of Dallas joining the NBA as an expansion team. They were entitled to choose one player from each team. The Sixers exposed Doug Collins, Henry Bibby, Jim Spanarkel and a forward, Bernard Toone, for the expansion draft. Dallas took Spanarkel.

Now came the collegiate draft and the Sixers had the No. 8 selection, the result of that long-ago trade of Melvin Bennett to Indiana, back in 1976. The player the Sixers coveted most was a

115

guard named Andrew Toney, an unheralded high-school player from Birmingham, Alabama, who had gone to obscure Southwest Louisiana. That college team had never been on national TV, but all the scouts knew who Andrew Toney was.

The Sixers' superscout, Jack McMahon, had suffered a heart attack in the winter of 1980, and Matt Goukas had been brought down from the broadcast booth to take his place. Matty had watched Andrew in the Aloha Classic in Hawaii and came back with this report: "Offensively, he could be something very special."

The Sixers still needed help on the guard line, especially in terms of point production. Lionel Hollins was an outstanding defensive player and a solid playmaker, but he was not a great shooter. And with Doug Collins hurt again, the team sorely lacked outside shooting.

The morning before the draft, we flew Andrew in for a physical, and then kept him in a hotel. It was a brazen move on our part because the rest of the league knew just as well as we what a blazing point machine Andrew was. But we had checked with the other teams which were to draft ahead of us; usually, they'll level with you on these matters. The team that worried us the most was New Jersey. The Nets had both the sixth and seventh picks in the draft, but they needed a center and were going to take Mike Gminski of Duke and then a forward from North Carolina, Mike O'Koren, who was a Jersey boy and, they hoped, would be a draw at the gate. At the same time, the Nets knew what they were passing up in Andrew Toney, because when I called their GM, Charlie Theokas, he said: "It looks like you'll get Toney. I want you to know we're giving you an NBA title. When you win it, order a ring for me."

We got Andrew. And then, with our own first-round pick, we took Monti Davis, a rebounding and scoring forward from Tennessee State. He, too, was thought to be special. Well, like they say in this business, it ain't an exact science. Monti Davis was one we'd just as soon forget.

Still, we felt we had made enough progress to stay ahead of the Celtics. But on the same day, in one great coup, they acquired

116

7-foot Robert Parish from the Golden State Warriors and drafted 6-11 Kevin McHale. Both those acquisitions were made for the sole purpose of combating the 76ers. In the playoffs, when the Sixers had humiliated the Celtics, it had been largely due to the play of the Twin Towers. Philly had dominated Boston inside. Now the Celtics had countered that. The great chess game continued . . . .

8

The Pits

BASKETBALL TALENT SCOUTS are forever searching for players with instant acceleration. The game is predicated on speed, of course, but not so much straight-ahead sprinting as quickness. And that was the attribute which so endeared Andrew Toney to the 76ers . . . his first step. It is cobra-quick, and it propels him around the unfortunate who is defending against him faster than a hiccup. In the NBA, they talk about isolating one player on another, and then "breaking down your man." It is the essence of the game, all the subtleties stripped away. One-on-one. In such duels, Andrew Toney is literally unstoppable.

So in the summer of 1980, the Sixers were able to find solace in the wake of their playoff loss to Los Angeles in the prospect of adding Toney to an already solid roster. The first step had been accomplished. But drafting Andrew was one thing; actually signing him was going to be quite another. As the No. 8 pick in the entire draft, he wasn't thinking small in contractual terms. Originally, he was going to be represented by a familiar name, Herb Rudoy, and negotiations might have been a bit easier. But he changed his mind and hired Bob Wright, a lawyer from Lafayette, Louisiana. This was Wright's first basketball player. He was a high-powered

Southern attorney, influential, and accustomed to high-stakes dealing, having represented a number of oil companies. The Sixers quickly discovered how much clout Wright wielded when he flew into Philadelphia in a private Lear jet. There was a considerable gap between what Andrew had in mind, monetarily, and what the Sixers were offering. Andrew did not sign.

He missed rookie camp, a camp which was dominated by Earl Cureton, whom the Sixers had drafted from the University of Detroit as a junior-eligible in 1979. Earl was intense, a springy leaper, a hustler, and he impressed the coaching staff. He would win a spot on the roster and remain a useful utility man, one of those good soldiers who fill whatever role they are assigned, and do so without complaint. That was the good news from rookie camp. The bad news was the other first-round selection—Monti Davis. He reported out of shape, was listless, lethargic, completely over-whelmed. All of the potential and promise he had shown in college seemed to have mysteriously evaporated. After the first day, Billy Cunningham said: "You'd better talk to that kid and tell him he won't drift through my camp. If he thinks he's got the team made just because he was a first-rounder, he's got another think coming." I tried scolding, pleading, coaxing, reasoning, and none of them worked. A few weeks into the season, Monti Davis would be waived.

Andrew, meanwhile, remained in Louisiana. In all my time with the NBA, he was the first holdout I'd been involved with, and I wasn't quite sure how to handle the situation. Finally, two hours before training camp was due to open, I called Wright and asked permission to talk to Andrew. I told Andrew I understood he plan-ned to go to graduate school and I just wanted to wish him luck with his studies, and it was unfortunate that he wasn't going to have a career with the Sixers. I wished him well, with my tongue imbedded in my cheek. It was a calculated gamble, and a con-siderable bluff. It worked, however. Almost immediately after I hung up, the phone rang and it was Bob Wright, saying: "All right, your strategy worked. I just heard from Andrew. We're flying in to Philly to sign."

John Langel, one of Fitz Dixon's attorneys, and I met Wright and Toney at the airport. Every other member of the Sixers family was already at Franklin and Marshall in Lancaster. We concluded negotiations and then I took Andrew out to dinner at the Fish Market, only to discover that he didn't like fish. (A year later I would take another first-round pick to dinner and an order of seafood would turn out to be almost fatal.) Andrew stayed at our house in Moorestown that night, and I've always felt you can tell a lot about people by the way kids react to them. Ours, especially Karyn, who was a year old at the time, really took to him.

The next morning we drove to camp. During the two-hour trip, Andrew managed about a dozen sentences. He's a quiet person by nature, but now he was nervous, anxious, worried about what sort of reception he was going to get, not only as a rookie but as a holdout who was showing up late.

He got out of the car, changed clothes, and immediately proceeded to go out and win the mile run, one of the staples of training camp. He won it in record time. In the drills that night, he showed his whole arsenal—knocking down long jumpers, driving with that tough-minded persistence of his, that utter fearlessness. Andrew is probably a better shooter when he is falling down, off balance, and blanketed by three defenders, than when he has an uncontested, wide-open shot. That is a special gift, and it requires a unique tunnel vision, an enormous power of concentration. Andrew plays as if he has blinders on, as though he is oblivious to any outside pressures. He did have a tendency to get out of control, and is still learning to harness himself, but it was obvious immediately that he was something special. The guard line, a source of so much concern for the last two years, looked potent and promising.

It was bolstered even more by the return of Doug Collins, who was making yet another comeback, and, in fact, had regained his starting job. But then, in the first exhibition game, against the Nets, Andrew twisted his ankle. It was a nasty sprain, and would force him to miss all of the preseason and the first month of the regular season. Still, the Sixers had Mo Cheeks, Lionel Hollins, Clint Richardson and Doug Collins, so Andrew's injury was not as crippling—to the team—as it would have been in the past. Henry Bibby had been waived at the end of camp, time finally having caught up with him. Henry was a gutsy little guy who had carved out a 9-year professional career for himself with limited skills, fortified by John Wooden's coaching at UCLA. He would do whatever was asked of him. He landed in San Diego, played out the 1980-81 season, then retired and got into coaching. Interestingly, Henry would end up at Arizona State, as an assistant there, along with Doug Collins.

Doug had rehabilitated himself from his latest injury and returned to play 12 games. But then, before Thanksgiving, his feet rebelled yet one more time at the pell-mell pace he demanded from them, and they gave out. He was back in the hospital.

All those years of uncertainty and injuries had taken a toll on the relationship between Doug and Billy Cunningham. Doug interpreted Billy's singlemindedness as a lack of personal interest in him. Billy respected what Doug had done, and all he had gone through, but he knew that every time Doug returned it was hold-your-breath waiting for the next inevitable injury. So this time, Doug said: "That's it. I'm retiring." But his injuries healed, as they always did, and around playoff time he got the fever to play again. At the end of the regular season, I had to meet him, in the Mount Laurel Hotel, and tell him that we just couldn't take a chance and activate him. Once the playoffs begin, your roster is frozen, so that if someone is injured he cannot be replaced. We just couldn't take the gamble of putting Doug on the roster, trimming an able body, and then have Doug go down again, with no replacement. He was understandably disappointed, but he took it well. He concentrated instead on his radio and TV work, which he had been doing for us, and that has led him into extensive exposure with CBS.

The regular season progresses and Andrew recovers from his ankle sprain, so at least we don't have to haggle our way through the trade market again. Andrew has one other thing going for him besides his talent—his temperament. He would make a mistake and Billy would stomp a fandango of rage and shriek his name in disgust. It reverberated all over every arena in the NBA. "Andre-w-w-w-w-w-w-w-w-w-w-w-w-w-w-w!" And out came Billy's hook and out came Andrew from the game, to sit on the bench and serve penance and reflect on his sins. To his credit, there was not an ounce of prima donna in Andrew. He'd slap his hands together in self-recrimination as though saying, "You dummy, what'd you do that for?" And then he would take his seat and listen to Billy's instructions and nod his understanding. A lot of other players would have sulked, pouted, brooded. But Andrew was—and is—responsive, eager to learn, highly coachable. There are other players who would have reacted to Billy's lash with a tart rebuttal, or who would have fomented dissension in the locker room. But Andrew understood that Billy's passion was so high where he was concerned because Billy saw in him such immense potential.

The Sixers have another outstanding regular season, even more successful than the year before. They win 62 games, lose only 20, a three-game improvement over the preceding season, and *that* one had been considered glittering. Along the way, Julius Erving is simply superb. He averages almost 25 points a game and wins the MVP award, one of the few noncenters so honored in the league's history. At the postseason banquet honoring Doc, Commissioner Larry O'Brien says: "Julius Erving is a national treasure, to be admired and savored."

But for all of their achievements, the Sixers finish another incredible race with Boston in a flat-footed tie. The Celtics also go 62-20. It comes down to the final game of the regular season, in Boston Garden, and the Celts beat the Sixers, 98-94, despite 35 points from Andrew Toney. It earns Boston the bye in the first round of the playoffs, and also the home court advantage, which will turn out to be prophetic.

So the Sixers become one of the few teams to win over 60 in one year, and still end up facing a miniseries, which is always a terrifying proposition because one off-night can be enough to render an entire season meaningless. The first round opponent is Indiana, and the Sixers win both games easily. In the Eastern Conference semifinals, Boston breezes through Chicago in four straight while the Sixers are locked in a seven-game gut-buster with Milwaukee. That is a tough Bucks team, with ageless Bob Lanier dragging his size 18½-EEE sneakers up and down the court with remarkable mobility, flanked by players like Marques Johnson, Sidney Moncrief and Junior Bridgeman, who is regarded during this season, along with Bobby Jones, as the best sixth man in basketball. The series rocks back and forth, an emotional yo-yo, and comes down to Game 7, in the Spectrum, on Easter Sunday. The building, inexplicably, is not even half full. Fewer than 7,000 show up, an embarrassment. Those who do come witness a beauty, the Sixers prevailing by one lonesome point, 99-98. The crowd—or, rather, the lack of one—attracts more attention the next day than accounts of the game. And Fitz is miffed. He talks afterwards about selling the team, and his remarks are printed. Out in Huntingdon Valley, a businessman and a Sixers' season-ticket-holder named Harold Katz reads of Fitz's displeasure and instructs his attorney, Laurence Shaiman, to contact Dixon and find out if he merely made a chance remark in a moment of pique, or if he is serious about selling the team. No one else is aware of this conversation, of course.

Out West, meanwhile, the defending champions have been ousted. The Lakers are upset by Houston and Moses Malone, and Houston continues on to beat Kansas City and San Antonio. Houston has qualified for the finals and everything seems to be breaking just right for the Sixers. The Rockets have been mostly lucky, and everyone agrees that the next champion of the NBA will come from the East.

Which means the survivor of Boston-Philadelphia.

The Celtics home-court advantage disappears the very first game. In the Garden, the Sixers win, 105-104, as Andrew Toney, who appears as though he doesn't know that he is supposed to be paralyzed by the pressure, calmly deposits two free throws in the closing seconds. Boston wins the next night by 19, and the series, tied, shifts to the Spectrum. The Sixers win by 10 and then by two, the latter sealed by Bobby Jones' defensive hustle and timely steal at the end. So now the Sixers are ahead, 3-1. Only one more win, and three games to do it in, and a weak Houston team—all that stands between them and that rainbow they have been chasing for so long. Every omen seems bursting with ripe promise.

It is, instead, the Sixers who burst.

They come apart at the seams, and it is recorded as one of the more memorable collapses in sports history. They will lose all three remaining games. Worse, they will have the lead going into the final minutes of each one, and they will not be able to hold it.

They are like a drowning man clutching at a razor blade.

In the entire previous history of NBA playoffs, only three times before had a team overcome a 3-1 deficit to capture a series. The Celtics, in the spring of 1981, will become the fourth. And yet, strangely, outside of Boston, this result is portrayed not so much as an heroic comeback by the Celtics as it is Philadelphia's past anguishes that cause the recorders of history to dwell more on the Sixers' defeat than on the Celtics' triumph.

Or maybe it is simply human nature to find more fascination in tragedy than in achievement.

Whatever, these are three dates that will live in infamy: APRIL 29, 1981—Game 5, Boston Garden, a Wednesday night. The Sixers are leading big and there are dwindling minutes remaining in the game. It looks like Philly will hand Boston its second straight 4-1 whipping in the playoffs. In fact, the fans are streaming out of the Garden in an early exodus of concession and some of them are stopping to shake my hand, offer their congratulations. "Good luck against Houston," they say. "Hope you win it all now." But down on the floor, the Sixers are unraveling in a rash of turnovers, dribbling the ball off their feet and out of bounds. The game that is won, the series that is over, suddenly isn't. Final score: Boston 111, Philadelphia 109.

MAY 1, 1981—Game 6, the Spectrum, a Friday night. Game 5 has been rationalized away as token resistance by the Celtics. No problem now, though, because the Sixers are in their own building. Sure enough, Philly shoots out of the starting blocks and storms to a huge lead by halftime. The champagne is on ice. In the second half, the Sixers melt faster than the ice. Boston chips away at the lead, ties it, goes ahead, and the panic is etched on the faces of the Sixers.

More turnovers, more lost possessions. They are struggling now to get off a shot. The Celtics lead and Andrew Toney, with the clock only a few ticks away from all zeroes, drives through a thicket of defenders and launches one of those impossible shots that he always makes. Except Kevin McHale rises up and blocks it. Then Cedric Maxwell makes two free throws with only two seconds left. Final Score: Boston 100, Philadelphia 98.

MAY 3, 1981—Game 7, Boston Garden, a Sunday afternoon. There is probably no more difficult arena in sports for a visiting team to win in than here; yet the Sixers, for the third straight game, start strong and assume immediate control. Until the closing minutes, and then the Celtics make another surge. I never am able to sit during a playoff game, but this day it is as though I have an army of fire ants in my shorts. I pace and rave to myself and try to walk off the tension up on the concourse, sneaking peeks as the action resumes. The pressure has gripped both teams and sucked the accuracy from their shooting arms. Neither team can make a basket. The Sixers manage one free throw by Mo Cheeks to cut Boston's lead to one point, after Larry Bird kisses a jumpshot off the glass, banking it in. The Sixers have the ball, but there is hardly any time left, no more than one second's worth. Philly calls time to set up one last desperate attempt. I remember going into a broom closet then and actually praying for some sort of miracle. From mid-court, out of bounds, Bobby Jones launches a high, arching pass toward the basket, hoping that somehow, some way, Doc will be able to climb an invisible rope and ram it through the basket. The Celtics, of course, are crowded under the basket, and there is a mass leap for the ball, which is still caroming around at the final buzzer. Final score: Boston 91, Philadelphia 90.

Three straight losses, by a total of five points. This is, indeed, The Pits.

Billy Cunningham's face is bloodless, agony digging ruts and creases across his forehead, gouging out pockets of frustration around his mouth. He is unable to speak. The players file into the Sixers locker room robot-like, dazed. Automatons, they dress out of habit and climb aboard the charter bus, which begins rocking wildly as it is attacked by crazed, delirious Celtics' fans.

The trip home should be called the Flight of Purgatory I.

The title that is just lying there, waiting to be grabbed, is seized by Boston. The Celtics beat Houston and Moses Malone. It goes six games, but Boston snuffs the Rockets in the final two, by 29 points and by 11.

The Sixers have plumbed new depths of frustration . . . .

There is one redeeming aspect of sports, and it is this: There is always another season.

The building is never complete, the quest never ends. Mercifully, there is always another draft to prepare for, so there is always enough work to occupy your thoughts and lessen the time of grieving.

The Sixers have five major bird dogs on whom they rely for information about college prospects—Bob Luksta in Chicago, Toby Kimball in San Diego, Sheridan James in San Francisco, Bud Olsen in Louisville, and Joe Ash in New York. Jack McMahon then sees all the top prospects in an effort to rank them for the draft.

In June of 1981, the general assumption was that the Sixers would take a forward. Steve Mix, Doc and Bobby Jones weren't getting any younger. The top three forwards that season coming out of college who might be available to us were Gene Banks of Duke, Jay Vincent of Michigan State and Howard Wood of Tennessee. But there was no unanimity among our scouts on which player had the most promise. However, the only player we all agreed on who appeared as though he would still be available when it was time for the Sixers to draft was not a forward but a quick little guard out of Cleveland State. Franklin Edwards. All the scouts liked him.

There was one other possibility, and that was Danny Ainge, who had enjoyed a good but not great career at Brigham Young. But his stock had shot up dramatically during the NCAA tournament. On national television, against Notre Dame, he had dribbled from one end of the court to the other, through all five Irish defenders, and had lobbed in the winning basket at the buzzer.

127

Suddenly, he was cover-boy famous. He had already gained a measure of fame by being one of the first athletes to take advantage of a new rule that allowed you to be a professional in one sport while retaining your eligibility and amateur status in another. He had been signed by the Toronto Blue Jays of the American League and had actually played parts of two baseball seasons in the big leagues. Toronto projected him as their second baseman of the future.

I had talked with several old friends from my baseball days and it was their private opinion that Danny Ainge's baseball skills were limited, and they didn't think he had that glittering a future in the game. Ainge, for his part, had been insisting publicly that he wanted to concentrate on baseball and that he was not interested in the NBA. You never want to just pass over someone with obvious athletic skills, however, so I called Ainge and set up a meeting with him in Cleveland for May 15. Toronto was playing the Indians that night. I came into Cleveland early that day and met with Franklin Edwards, and then he drove me to the hotel where Ainge and the Blue Jays were staying. Danny was in his room, watching the afternoon soaps, and we had a long talk. He reminded me of Doug Collins in his enthusiasm. Finally, I asked him point-blank: "Look Danny, if we draft you, are we just wasting a first round pick?" He replied: "Yes. I want to concentrate on baseball, have an entire off-season to work on my hitting instead of playing basketball."

Just to be sure, I called him a second time, later, and he reiterated his position. The day of the draft, Boston picked Danny Ainge on the second round. He signed with them. Later, I found myself in the middle of a lawsuit, testifying in Toronto's behalf. They had sued Ainge for breach of contract. They felt he had misled them. I knew he had misled the Sixers. That trip to Cleveland had not been entirely a waste, however. Inadvertently, and quite by chance, I had left Ainge's hotel room and gone to the ballpark that night to watch the Indians-Blue Jays game. I sat behind the third base dugout and kept score, which I normally don't do. Along about the sixth inning, I looked at my scorecard and realized this was history. That night, Len Barker of the Indians

Julius Erving takes time to bring some joy into the life of a handicapped youngster. Erving is a gracious, caring person who gives of himself to many worthy causes. Despite his world-wide fame, Dr. J. remains a soft spoken, humble Christian gentleman.

Maurice Cheeks visited this delighted youngster at Philadelphia's Children's Hospital at Christmas 1979. All of the Sixer players spend quality time at schools, hospitals, and clinics throughout the Delaware Valley.

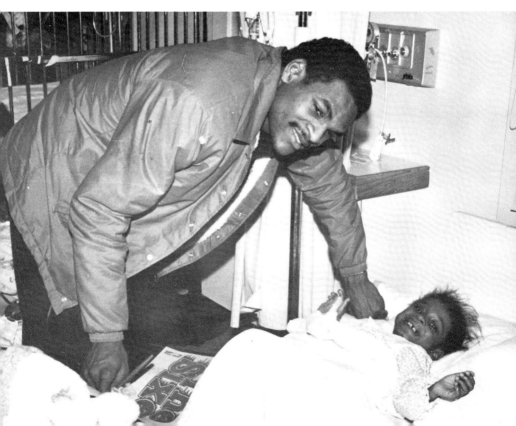

This was a "Fine and Dandy" day for the Sixers as Pat Williams announces that Andrew Toney is the Sixers first round pick in 1980. Billy Cunningham (left) and owner Fitz Dixon nod their approval. Dixon developed a deep interest in the 76ers and loved moments like this when he felt like "one of the boys." Many observers felt that Dixon's main athletic loves were the riding career of his daughter, Ellin, and the football fortunes at the Eagles, Temple, Widener, and Episcopal Academy. (By the way, you never know what the NBA draft will bring. The Sixers fifth round pick in 1981 was Steve Craig of Brigham Young who married Marie Osmond a year later.)

Billy Cunningham has become a master at dealing with the press and patiently answering their questions. At a major press conference in mid June 1983, Billy discusses his new three year contract to continue as the 76ers head coach. Billy has developed into one of the NBA's outstanding coaches.

This is the 1966-67 76ers championship club at a reunion in 1980 after being named the greatest NBA team in history.
1st row (L to R) Wilt Chamberlain, Dave Gambee, Luke Jackson, Billy Cunningham, and Chet Walker. 2nd row (L to R) Trainer Al Domenico, Dr. Stanley Lorber, coach Alex Hannum, Wali Jones, Billy Melchionni, Matt Guokas, Hal Greer, Larry Costello, and owner Irv Kosloff. Kos is a genuine basketball fan and said on many occasions his first desire would have been to be a pro player, then a pro coach, then the general manager, and then the owner. Said Kös, "The owner gets all the blame if things go wrong and none of the credit if they go right."

Hal Greer (left) and Wilt Chamberlain reminisce at the Ovations club at the Spectrum in 1980. Both players were vital cogs in the great 1967 Sixers team and went on to become members of the Basketball Hall of Fame in Springfield, Mass.

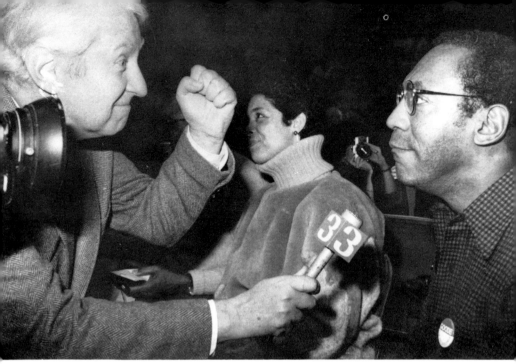

MIKE MAIC

Bob Bradley (left), popular sports announcer for Channels 3 and 17, interviews Bill
Cosby at a Sixers game. Cosby, a Philadelphia native, is a loyal 76ers fan who follows
the team faithfully. When the 76ers hosted the NBA All-Star Game in 1976, Cosby was
the featured speaker at the pre-game banquet. He delivered a spontaneous 45 minute
routine that had 'em rolling in the aisles.

The 76ers' wildest fan is Steve Solms (standing right), a wealthy real estate tycoon
in center city Philadelphia. You'd never know it at a Sixers game; he sits front row
center court, across from the Sixers bench, and goes absolutely bananas when the
76ers go on a tear.

MIKE MAICHER

The one and only Dave Zinkoff in action behind the mike. Club president Lou Scheinfeld made a major mistake in releasing Zink in 1980. A pro basketball game in Philadelphia is incomplete without Zink's voice booming through the Spectrum.

Before every "Big" Sixer home game, Grover Washington, Jr. takes center stage to play the national anthem on his famous saxophone. Grover is such a devoted fan he plans his world wide concert tours around the Sixers' home schedule.

Celebrities follow the 76ers everywhere the team goes. Rev. Jesse Jackson stops by the locker room for a post game visit with owner Harold Katz.

Coach Gene Shue (right) and owner Fitz Dixon enjoy a pleasant moment together after Fitz bought the 76ers in 1976. However, there was always a strain between the two men and when the Sixers got off to a staggering start in November 1977, Shue was replaced by Billy Cunningham.

Hunter McMullin dances
with Mrs. Bill Campbell at
a Sixers team party.
McMullin was taught and
coached at Episcopal
Academy by Fitz Dixon in
the '50's before becoming a
Philadelphia stock broker.
In 1975 McMullin was
hired by Dixon to help run
the Wings lacrosse team
before joining the Sixers in
1976.

This is a photo you won't
see on the society pages of
the Philadelphia Inquirer!
Fitz Dixon's tall, stately
wife Edith, cuts loose on
the dance floor with the
master of swing, Darryl
Dawkins.

Fitz Dixon nicknamed Darryl Dawkins "Shorty". At the team Christmas party in 1978, Fitz climbed on a chair to look big Darryl in the eye. Normally a very reserved, proper man, Dixon relished this type of occasion when he could let his hair down. Dixon also became a vocal rooter and referee baiter from his front row seat near the Sixers' bench.

One of Harold Katz's first acts as owner in July 1981 was to retain Pat Williams (right) as general manager. There was one stipulation, however. Said Katz, "Pat, you can run any promotions you want except that lousy trained pig act." At the press conference announcing Williams' rehiring, farmer Dave Bailey of Alloway, New Jersey presents Katz with a freshly scrubbed pig named "Harold."

On November 13, 1979 Darryl Dawkins electrified the basketball world when he shattered the backboard at Kansas City's Municipal Auditorium in a game against the Kings. Otis Birdsong (10) watches in stunned disbelief. The Sixers drafted Dawkins out of high school in 1975 and were tempted to do it again in 1976 with Darrell Griffith of Louisville, KY. They scouted him all winter but decided at the last minute he wasn't mature enough.

Julius Erving mounts a camel on his 1981 trip to Israel. Dr. J. is a world-wide figure and instantly recognized almost everywhere he goes.

Anything for a little publicity! The Sixers' Steve Mix mounts an elephant outside the Spectrum to join a parade promoting the opening of the Circus.

Center Mark McNamara ends up with a 7 foot boa constrictor around his neck at the press conference in 1982 announcing his signing as the 76ers first pick. McNamara, an avid outdoorsman, kept two pet snakes in his room while a student at California-Berkley.

YOSSI ROTH

The Sixers staged a ladies mud wrestling contest following a Spectrum game in March 1982. The final bout featured sportscaster Howard Eskin pinning two enormous women at one time and then raising his arms in triumph. Needless to say, this is an athletic activity that would not have been displayed during the Dixon era.

Izzy, one of the Sixers most unusual fans, shows up at every home game without a ticket, talks his way past the guards, and then entertains the crowd at time outs with his unusual assortment of dance steps.

MIKE MAICHER

Moses Malone celebrated his 28th birthday at the Spectrum before a game in 1983. Moses is quiet and reserved but the presentation of this enormous cake really excited him.

Don Nelson, Milwaukee Bucks Coach, erupted in a fit of rage at a referee's call in January 1983, and threw his sports jacket to the center of the Spectrum floor. Thus the stage was set for the "Don Nelson Coat Throwing Contest" when the Bucks returned in March. This fan fires Nelson's tattered jacket almost 50 feet down the floor to capture first prize as Big Shot looks on approvingly.

Krazy George is a nomadic ball handling whiz who entertains basketball fans across America. Part of his act is this enormous ball which finds its resting place on the Spectrum rim.

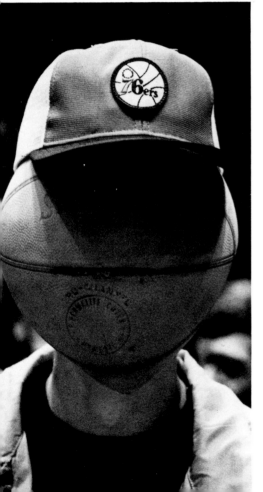

Wherever Pat Williams goes to operate a team, Victor, the Wrestling Bear, is sure to follow as a lively halftime attraction. Victor is a six foot, 600 pound bruiser who hates to lose. Needless to say, he loses very few bouts.

Pro basketball fans in Philadelphia come in all shapes, sizes, and styles. This one came and left his head at home.

Billy Cunningham is an avid follower of all sports even though most of his spare time is spent with wife Sondra and their two daughters. In 1980 Billy participated in a celebrity softball game before a Phillies-Dodgers game at Veterans Stadium.

Julius Erving and George McGinnis were Sixer teammates in 1976-77 and 1977-78. Here they team up for a guest special on the Mike Douglas Show when it originated from Philadelphia.

The Sixers NBA Championship was highlighted on June 8, 1983 by a ten minute ceremony in the Rose Garden with President Ronald Reagan. NBA Commissioner Lawrence O'Brien presents the President with a NBA referee's jacket. The attentive Sixers are (L to R): Marc Iavaroni, Clemon Johnson, Bobby Jones, Billy Cunningham, and Julius Erving.

OFFICIAL WHITE HOUSE PHOTO

ended up pitching a perfect game against Toronto.

Anyway, the 76ers made Franklin Edwards their first pick in the 1981 draft. His agent was Ron Grinker of Cincinnati, who had been so helpful for us when we were acquiring Mo Cheeks, and Franklin was signed quickly. We flew him into town so he could be rushed into Baker League play and spend the summer gaining game experience. He signed in the afternoon and I took him to dinner at Billy Cunningham's hotel that evening. He had flounder stuffed with crabmeat. Halfway through the game that night, he collapses on the bench, his eyes swelling almost shut and his entire body puffing up grotesquely. He is rushed, on a stretcher, to Temple Hospital.

The diagnosis: An allergic reaction, a violent one. Franklin Edwards is allergic to shellfish. The flounder was safe, but the crabmeat stuffing was very nearly a killer. We almost lost our No. 1 pick before he spent his first 24 hours in town . . . .

All through the spring and early summer of 1981, the Sixers' owner had been invisible. Fitz Dixon had been devastated by the playoff failure against Boston, so embarrassed that it was as though he had gone into a monastic retreat. We usually talked two-three times a week, and I hadn't heard from him since May 4. Now it was the summer and I was up in the Adirondack Mountains for some summer basketball camps, and on an island out in the middle of Schroon Lake I get a phone call from Hunter McMullin.

"It's in your best interests," he says, "to come back to Philadelphia as quickly as possible."

"Why?"

"I can't say."

"Oh, come on, Hunter . . . ."

"Sorry, I just can't."

Remember that Hunter and I had started out five years before with that memorable "meet-your-new-owner" greeting which had been followed by Hunter McMullin's smug: "And when did *you* find out about the sale?" We had come, however, to a closer relationship, thrown together in the same foxhole when Fitz Dixon had brought in Lou Scheinfeld. Halfway through the 1980-81 season, Fitz had quietly told Scheinfeld that his contract would not be renewed. Lou had not bound up the old wounds but had opened new ones during his brief tenure. Three weeks after our collapse against Boston, he had called the staff together and, emotionally, informed them he wouldn't be returning. When he had first taken over, a couple of veteran Scheinfeld watchers, Claire Rothman, who helps run the Forum in LA, and Hal Freeman, who runs the Philadelphia Civic Center, had told me: "Hang in there; he'll last two years, tops." They had been right; his era had lasted a year and a half.

Now Hunter McMullin is calling me in the middle of nowhere, obviously trying to warn me about something, but he is vague about what is happening. So I call Irv Kosloff.

"Kos, what's up?"

"Well, Fitz has negotiated the sale of the 76ers."

"So who's the new owner?"

"A man named Harold Katz."

"I never heard of him."

"Well, he's been a season-ticket-holder. He looks a lot like Irwin Weiner."

I grabbed the next plane out, early the following morning, and flew to Philadelphia. There, in the Philadelphia Sheraton Hotel, fifteen minutes before Harold Katz was to be introduced at a press conference, I met him for the first time.

Kos was right. I recognized him. I always make it a practice to stand out in the hallways of the Spectrum and watch the people, and I realized I had seen Harold Katz countless times coming and going from Sixers games.

There is a lesson to be learned there: Always be kind to your season-ticket-holders, for one day they may be your owner.

This new owner is a self-made multi-multi-multi-millionaire, a South Philadelphia street kid who is a basketball fanatic. This is obviously a moment of great triumph for him, but there are a million thoughts swirling through his mind, and he seems very subdued. I am appointed to introduce the new owner to the media, a man I have now known for all of a quarter of an hour.

The press conference goes well. There is a warm family scene, with Harold introducing his wife, Barbara, and his children. I return to basketball camp, and when I get back to Philadelphia, the newspapers are filled with rumors that I'm leaving, the most prominent landing spots being the Chicago White Sox or the Cubs. I did, in fact, hear from Eddie Einhorn, the Sox owner, about a possible job there.

But a week later, I had a long, five-hour meeting with the Sixers' new owner, who was a stark contrast to Fitz Dixon. We were like a couple of street dogs sniffing, each trying to figure out the other. Harold had strong opinions, was very aggressive, and obviously was hooked on the game, absorbed by it. Every player who was brought up, he was totally conversant about. Many owners of professional sports teams have them strictly as hobbies; it was plain that here was an owner with a more than passing interest in his new acquisition. He asked me how I would set up the organization and I replied I felt the best structure was one man in charge, reporting directly to the owner. He agreed, to a point.

"I want to see you in action," he said.

He had set up a meeting the following day with Mayor William Green, trying to seek some relief, some mayoral intervention, from that strangling Spectrum lease, and also inquiring about beefed-up security from city police. He said he would pick me up, which he did, in a limousine that looked to be about a block and a half long. I climb in and Harold is waving that day's papers. The headlines say that his wife has sued him to prevent him from buying the team, from selling any of his holdings; she has filed for divorce. Clearly, this is not going to be a low-profile stewardship.

So we go to City Hall and walk into Green's office, and Harold, brandishing the papers, opens with: "Mayor, you oughta love me. I'm keeping you off the front pages."

And the mayor responds with a warm handshake and: "Harry, how are you?"

Stricken, Harold says: "Mayor, it's Harold . . . *Harold!*"

Later, I have one more long meeting with Harold, and I am

131

beginning to feel more comfortable. He wants to hire John Nash away from the Big Five, which is fine with me. John is a good man, with excellent credentials, someone I feel I can work with.

Harold Katz is a marketing genius and he knows promotions. He also knows promotions are my specialty. "I'll give you a free hand in that area," he says. "But with one stipulation—no pigs." This alludes to one of my all-time fiascos, of which there will be more detail later.

A press conference is set up to announce my retention as general manager and to introduce John Nash as the business manager of the 76ers. It is going to receive a lot of coverage: every move the Sixers make at this point gets ink because this is a silent summer, the year of the baseball strike. I call a friend of mine, Dave Bailey, who owns a farm in Alloway, New Jersey, and ask him to bring a piglet to the Quality Inn the next day. Mind you, I'm still uncertain about Harold Katz's sense of humor, but Dave, all decked out in farmer's bib overalls and straw hat, marches down the aisle at the press conference, on my cue, with this freshly scrubbed, squealing pig under his arm, and presents it to Harold.

I tell the writers, who ask about details of my contract, that Harold had instructed me to reveal none of the terms because he is as ashamed of it as I am. I say that I have a signing bonus that will allow my mother to work the rest of her life. I say that he has signed me to a multi-day deal, and that Harold Katz' idea of an obscene gesture is reaching for the check.

Now I'm wondering if I have also just authored my own obituary with the 76ers. I sneak a peek at Harold, and to my considerable relief, he is loving it. In fact, whenever we appear together at a public function afterwards, he says: "Rip me, rip me." I feel like Don Rickles. I also feel rejuvenated and relieved . . . .

Harold had met with Hunter McMullin and they agreed he wouldn't be staying on under the new regime, though it would still be a few weeks before the sale was completed and League approval of the new owner secured. There was a meeting to introduce the new staff, and just before it began here came Hunter striding down

132

the hallway. He didn't know about the meeting, but when he saw all the people gathering, he automatically headed for it. I knew it would be a disaster if he got in there, an embarrassment to him and to Harold. So here came Hunter, pipe ablaze, this balding, duck-walking, prototype latterday Main Line preppie with argyle socks and penny loafers, accustomed to summering in Maine, and there is no time for me to explain, so I head him off at the pass. I just stepped in front of him, blocked his entrance, and closed the door. I knew it was abrupt, but it was all I could think of to do to head off what would have been an uncomfortable confrontation.

After the staff meeting, I went to Hunter's office to explain, but he wanted no part of an explanation, nor of me. He was enraged, so angry that he couldn't speak. His face was flushed and the more he looked at me, the deeper the flush, until it went from red almost to purple. I tried to talk to him twice more, and then he left for vacation, and I mailed him a note of apology and explanation, but never heard back from him.

Hunter and I had had our run-ins before. Once, he had come into my office and slammed down a dictionary on my desk and thundered: "Why don't you look up the word 'communicate'?" And then he stormed out. Another time, he said: "You know, I've read your book (*The Gingerbread Man*, an autobiography published 10 years ago) and it sure doesn't correlate with the way you're dealing with me." Now that really stung. In a lot of that book I talk about my Christian beliefs and applying them to relationships. But over the years, Hunter and I had resolved our differences . . . until the day I shut the door on him and never got to explain why. . . .

There was one other farewell that had to be said that summer. Fitz Dixon.

He had just dropped out of sight. He hadn't attended the press conference in July, when Harold was introduced as the new owner. I called him at his estate in Maine, told him I was sorry about the playoff loss, told him I was sorry he was getting out.

Fitz had always backed us fiercely. He was a real competitor. Most owners, after a month, know everything. But in his five years

Fitz had never pretended to be a basketball expert. Whatever resources the team needed, he would provide. He wanted to bring a championship to Philadelphia badly, and whatever player we suggested, he was willing to open his checkbook without hesitation. But the financial losses he was suffering from the 76ers had been mounting, and finally it seemed his spirit had been broken. He just couldn't see any hope of ever attaining that championship. Something would always go wrong. And so, with sadness, he was bowing out.

9

Almost To The Mountaintop

ON WEDDING DAYS there are no ugly brides, and on draft days there are no bad choices; in the mind of the team that is drafting, every pick is swift, strong and springy. Draft day is when you let your optimism run wild. Nonetheless, it is always comforting to find out that your No. 1 *can* play. And that's what the 76ers learned, to their relief, in the training camp of 1982. Franklin Edwards is going to make the team and he is going to help, not so much this season as next.

Just prior to that camp, a familiar figure had come, wrenchingly, to the end of the line. Doug Collins had been working out on his own all summer, trying to coax one more miracle out of his ravaged feet and legs. There was simply no room for him on the 76ers roster, but Chicago had indicated they might be willing to take a chance on him. And then, in another one of those freakish mishaps that plagued Doug, he made a move in a scrimmage and his good knee collapsed. The trade to Chicago was aborted. Doug still had four years left on his Sixers' contract, so he was put to work in public relations, front office administration, and in radio and TV broadcasting. On the side, he became a volunteer assistant coach at Penn, and both those careers have since blossomed; he is coaching at Arizona State and did this year's playoffs for CBS-TV. There definitely is life after basketball for Doug Collins.

At the Sixers' preseason camp, meanwhile, it is hardly things as usual. The new owner, a man worth hundreds of millions of dollars, sits on the bleachers every day, in sweatsuit and sneakers, kibitzing, analyzing every play, obviously relishing his new role. Harold Katz is grooving on basketball. Every session is a feast. When the season begins, he will come down from his plush super-box after every game and huddle behind closed doors with Billy Cunningham, replaying every minute. It is not interference, not meddling; it is just that Harold is hopelessly hooked on the game and takes a genuine interest in his team. "He is," says Billy, admiringly, "an intense competitor."

The twelfth, and final, spot on that roster goes to Ollie Johnson, who had starred at Temple and carved out a 10-year career for himself in the NBA. The Sixers had picked him up halfway through the previous season and he had been a valuable spot player, especially as an outside shooter. He would spend the last part of the 1981-82 season on the injured list, although he wasn't really hurt. It was just that time had caught up with him, but, like Doug Collins, he had developed outside business interests and would be able to make the transition to the "real world" fairly smoothly.

The season begins amidst the usual turmoil in Cleveland, with the owner, Ted Stepien, again revving up his revolving door of players and coaches. Cleveland called and asked permission to talk to Chuck Daly, and ended up hiring him as their new coach. Chuck had served his apprenticeship and wanted, understandably, to get out on his own. We certainly didn't want to hold him back, but we did manage to extract from Cleveland a No. 2 pick in the 1985 draft in exchange for Chuck. Within 90 days, Chuck knew the situation was hopeless in Cleveland. He made a settlement on his contract and returned to the Sixers as part of the broadcast crew. But his heart remains in coaching, and he has all the credentials to be a successful head man somewhere in the NBA. When Chuck left for Cleveland, Matt Goukas came down from the booth and assumed his job as assistant coach to Billy. Like Chuck, Matty is a cinch to be a head coach in this league, and a good one. And Chuck, meanwhile, took the head coaching job at Detroit for the 1983-84 season.

On Sunday, January 9, 1982 in a game at New Jersey, Darryl Dawkins goes up for a jumpshot and as he comes down there is a slight, brushing contact between him and Mike Gminski. It looks harmless enough, but Darryl crumples to the floor. X-rays reveal a broken leg.

Darryl has been the Sixers' seven-year enigma, the child prodigy who never quite became the monster in the middle everyone had foreseen. Maybe he was a victim of everyone else's great expectations. Everyone had a theory about Darryl, and everyone had tried his theory. Harold Katz had joined that long line. He saw Darryl as a personal project. Harold is a shrewd motivator; but, like everyone before him, he found only frustration. Darryl would sparkle for brief stretches, and then just drift off. He was impossible to analyze. Before his broken leg, there had been talk of trading him.

Now Caldwell Jones, the quiet man, stiletto-slim, unemotional, reliable, was called on to play an even bigger role in the middle, and Earl Cureton moved up a notch in the rotation. The Sixers were forced to shop around for a center. In the meantime, a neon name from an earlier era surfaced—Wilt Chamberlain. He was 45 years old and 10 years out of the game, but Harold became enamored of the box office possibilities. Wilt, for his part, did nothing to dissuade all the speculation. He loved the attention. When things got dull, Wilt would periodically refocus the spotlight on himself by threatening to return to basketball. Harold Katz flew to Los Angeles, met with Wilt, and Wilt gave him more encouragement than discouragement.

This dragged on for two weeks, Wilt milking it, and it certainly did nothing to hurt the Sixers in terms of publicity. They were in the headlines every day. It was, of course, all a tease by Wilt, and he resolved it, finally, with a dramatic telegram to

Harold, turning him down. But there will surely come another year when Wilt will cast himself as bait once again, and somebody will bite and he will coyly string him along for another few days of ink.

In the meantime, the Sixers are roaming through the league, and the name of Mike Bantom crops up. Local player, having prepped at Roman Catholic; All-American at St. Joseph's; member of the 1972 Olympic team. He is with Indiana now and the Pacers are in financial trouble. In a late night call, they agree to send Philadelphia Mike Bantom in exchange for $100,000. Bantom isn't a center but he has experience, he can bang the boards, and he plays Larry Bird tougher than any other defender in the NBA. Mike makes some contributions, helps the team, but near the end of the season begins to flounder. In the playoffs, it appears that he has caught the George McGinnis disease. The Sixers release him in the summer of 1982 and he drifts over to Italy to play.

The Sixers go 58-24 in the 1981-82 season, again forging one of the best records ever, but Boston loses only 19 games and gets the bye in the playoffs while Philly must face another miniseries. This time the opponent is Atlanta, and the Sixers put the torch to the Hawks in the first game, winning by a whopping 35 points.

Game 2 is in Atlanta and it goes into overtime, the Sixers finally prevailing. But the highlight is Lionel Hollins and Atlanta's 7-foot, 1-inch center, Wayne (Tree) Rollins. Rollins throws a flagrant elbow and Hollins retaliates by hitting him on the back of his head. Rollins chases Hollins. The Tree after the Train. Round and round they go, behind the basket, down the aisle, into the seats, back out onto the floor. It is slapstick comedy, but it has some tragic overtones. Hollins has broken his hand on Rollins' head, and will miss the playoffs. (As evidence of how long the NBA playoffs last, Train will end up playing against Los Angeles in the finals.)

There is, however, something very favorable for the Sixers in all of this. Hollins' absence forces Billy Cunningham to elevate Andrew Toney to a starting position. Andrew responds magnificently, and this becomes the making of him into one of the league's premier guards. At the same time, Clint Richardson moves up to No. 3 and he, too, will deliver off the bench. In almost every game when Clint comes in, he makes an immediate impact, either defensively, scoring or rebounding. Andrew, of course, now will receive the minutes he has yearned for, and he will crank up some surreal nights.

In the quarterfinals, the Sixers meet Milwaukee and quickly open up a 3-1 lead. But they lose Game 5, in the Spectrum, and now must go back to Milwaukee, and there is the uneasy sensation that a series that began as a breeze is going to turn into a seventh-game white knuckler. But this Sixers team has a habit of doing what you least expect when you least expect it. They beat the Bucks in Milwaukee, on a Friday night. There is no time to savor it, however, because the Sixers must fly immediately to Boston to open the Eastern Conference finals that Sunday afternoon. They promptly get obliterated by the Celtics, losing by 40. Game 2, in Boston Garden, and the Sixers are at their schizophrenic best. The same team that was stampeded by 40 turns around and wins . . . and comes back to Philadelphia and promptly wins two more. The Sixers are up 3-1, just like the previous spring, and the Celtics cackle: "Now we got 'em right where we want 'em." Could it be *deja vu?* "Doesn't he play power forward for Paris?" cracks Darryl Dawkins.

So the Sixers are loose, confident there will be no repetition of the previous year's collapse. But Boston wins Game 5, forces Game 6 back in the Spectrum, and the Celtics' coach, Bill Fitch, says: "If we can win the next game and force this thing back to Boston, then Philadelphia will be so tight you won't be able to drive a needle up their you-know-what with a sledgehammer."

The Celtics do, indeed, win Game 6, and there is an ugly, ugly feeling inside the Spectrum that Friday night, a sense of betrayal. It's Write-Off City. Everyone believes this will be a carbon copy of last year, the Sixers blowing yet another 3-1 lead. One Philadelphia sports columnist, ahem, writes that the Sixers have been born under the sign of the accordion, that they are the NBA's version of the cliff divers of Acapulco, that they are now dead and burial will be under that parquet floor in Boston Garden that Sunday afternoon. The front page of one Boston paper asks, in war-sized type: "WILL

SIXERS CHOKE?" And the other Boston paper has a cartoon of Billy Cunningham, cold sweat pouring off his face, awakening from a nightmare, Scroogelike, and asking: "Ghosts . . . what ghosts?" All around him are sheeted, hooded demons labeled "Ghosts of Playoffs Past." And in the Garden that afternoon three Celtics fans parade through the howling arena, attired in sheets and other appropriate haunting togs.

But there is a resolve among the Sixers' players. They have been abandoned by everyone else, and now they are the lonely dozen, and somewhere they find a resolute purpose.

Later, Maurice Cheeks, trying to explain it, will say: "We had no one else to turn to but ourselves. We found strength in each other."

And so they did. They took command from the beginning and repulsed every Boston surge. The Sixers win, decisively, and rip the unjust monkey off their backs. History does not repeat. History reverses itself, instead.

In the process, the Sixers won much more than a game and a series. They won a city.

When their plane landed in Philadelphia that night, there was a joyous outpouring of fans, a roaring welcome at the airport. All was forgiven.

At that moment of ecstasy, that long-overdue *We Owe You One* seemed far, far away. Against all odds, they had overcome. It was too bad the season could not have ended right there. The finals could only be anticlimactic after that pulsating achievement in Boston.

But there they were, for the third time in six seasons, once again in the NBA finals, facing the Lakers, who were rested and ready, who had stormed through the first two rounds without a single defeat. LA mounted a third-quarter blitz in Game 1 and swept to its ninth straight playoff game victory, a record.

The Sixers rebounded to win Game 2, then traveled to the Coast and absorbed two whippings, with Bob McAdoo bedeviling them. His success was particularly frustrating for the Sixers because his agent had called Philly that winter. But it was around Christ-

140

mas time and the Sixers really had no opening on their roster at that point, not for a player who was considered a major risk, having come off three consecutive unproductive years. The Lakers had taken a chance on McAdoo out of desperation when one of their big men, Mitch Kupchak, was lost for the season with an injury. That had occurred not too long before Darryl Dawkins broke his leg. If the timing had been different by just a few days, McAdoo would have been playing for the Sixers.

Game 5 is back in Philadelphia, and even though the Lakers have lost only one of 12 playoff games, the Sixers show the same courage they had in Boston. They win, and now it is back for a sixth game, the Sixers refusing to go quietly into the night.

On the eighth of June, 1982, the latest the playoffs have ever gone, the Lakers win the title, their second in three years. Los Angeles 114, Philadelphia 104. Jamaal Wilkes scores 27 points and Magic Johnson hits three 13s—13 rebounds, 13 assists, 13 points. It is hardly an unlucky number for the Lakers.

Once more, the Sixers have been almost to the mountaintop, and once more they have fallen just short of the summit.

There is disappointment, of course, but it is not so deep this time. The 76ers have fought the good fight this time; they have been carried home on their shields again, but there is no disgrace, no galling sense of unfulfillment. Los Angeles has put together one of the most impressive playoff efforts in history; they are clearly the better team, and deserving champions. And, besides, on a memorable, glittering afternoon in Boston, the Sixers had earned for themselves a measure of redemption.

So they were not the champions. They were not winners. But neither were they perceived this time as losers. There was no humiliation.

This time, apologies were not necessary.

The marching orders for the summer of 1982 were clear and concise: Get rid of Darryl Dawkins.

His broken leg had mended and he had returned to play, but it

141

was with his usual inconsistency. He had also traded agents, leaving Herb Rudoy and going with Tom Meehan, and in February of 1982 had signed a five-year contract with the Sixers, who had agreed to that, however reluctantly, to prevent Darryl from becoming a free agent. His playoff performance had done nothing to enhance his market value, and that summer we dangled him in front of several teams, but were greeted with disinterest. The one nibble came from Utah, which was interested in Darryl and Lionel Hollins. They had the No. 3 pick in the 1982 draft, and we planned on using that to acquire Dominique Wilkins of Georgia, who was advertised as "The Human Highlights Film." But just before the draft, Utah turned us down.

We went into the draft with the 22nd pick overall and used it on Mark McNamara, a 7-footer from the University of California. He had led the Pac-10 Conference in rebounding *and* scoring, a rare double that had previously been accomplished only by Bill Walton and Kareem Abdul-Jabbar. We needed a trenchman, a banger inside. All during the previous season, Harold Katz had complained about the lack of physical play by the Sixers. "We lead the NBA in helping guys to their feet," he said. "We're too nice. We need to lead the NBA in knocking people down, not helping them up."

McNamara was a bright, articulate kid with an interest in wildlife, an interest which prompted him to have a couple of rather unique roommates—snakes. Mark's attorney was Steve Blick, and we reached an agreement by mid-July, and flew Mark into Philadelphia for introductions to the media. Remembering our success with Harold the Pig the summer before, I phoned the Philadelphia Zoo. And when Mark is introduced, I say we want to make him feel right at home, and he is presented with this very large python. The three city-bred people at the front table—Harold Katz of Philadelphia and Billy Cunningham and Jack McMahon of Brooklyn—are diving for the windows. Mark cradles the snake like it's a long-lost friend and wraps it around his neck. The picture makes every newspaper in the country.

Our two second-round picks in that draft are Mitchell Anderson of Bradley and Russ Schoene of Tennessee-Chattanooga, a couple of big, rangy forwards. They are the 36th and 45th picks overall, and rarely do selections that far down the list provide you with anything but bodies at training camp. But Schoene in particular will prove to be valuable the very next winter because he will enable us to acquire Clemon Johnson in a trade. Also, both Anderson and Schoene can be signed for relatively low salaries, the first fiscal move in a payroll-trimming effort that will ultimately lead to the acquisition of one Moses Malone.

Mark McNamara plays in the Los Angeles summer league, as does Franklin Edwards, and Matty Goukas is out there watching them. One day, Matty calls and says: "The most impressive player out here is Marc Iavaroni."

I remember the name. Big, strong, physical player. Was Virginia's center before Ralph Sampson. Tough rebounder. He had had some shots with other NBA teams but was released and then played for three seasons in Italy, where the style of play is not for the timid. We want him in our camp, but other NBA clubs have watched him and they covet him, too. Finally we offer to fly him in, fly him back to LA so he can get his camper and drive back, and we give him permission to miss the first day of rookie camp. He agrees, and he is impressive, a banger who does not shy away from elbows and knees. We sign him, although we have to guarantee some of his first year's contract.

Russ Schoene has an offer to play in Italy, but we sign him, too.

By now it is late summer and my wife and I are ready to join Doc and Turquoise and five other NBA players on one of those once-in-a-lifetime trips; two weeks in Mainland China. At the end of the trip, we finally reach a telephone, in Hong Kong, and phone home, from 6,000 miles away. There is, it turns out, a news bombshell to catch up on. Darryl Dawkins has been sent to the New Jersey Nets, for $600,000 and a 1983 first-round draft pick. It is August 27, 1982. Darryl Dawkins' departure has been inevitable, but when it becomes fact, I feel marooned, isolated; to learn of it in a time zone 12 hours away was a weird, empty sort of feeling.

143

That news is not exactly hailed in Philadelphia, because Darryl's departure comes not long after the 76ers have announced an across-the-board 45 percent increase in ticket prices for the 1982-83 season. The club is taking flak. Darryl's following had dwindled but he still drew people anxious to witness another shattered backboard and his psychedelic dunks. And the ticket price increase, along with the installation of $50-a-pop courtside seats, did not sit well with a public that was still waiting for a world title.

Now things get hectic. Doc and I are flying from Hong Kong to New York, a 24-hour trip with a stop only in Tokyo. Harold Katz is flying from Philadelphia to Reno for a short vacation. Billy Cunningham is on the golf course down in Pinehurst. But the only thing moving faster than the jet engines is the mind of Harold Katz. He has become obsessed with one player—Moses Malone—who is now a free agent. Moses Malone, two time MVP, the NBA's leading rebounder and leading scorer.

The plane touches down in Reno and Harold is on the phone back to John Nash in the Sixers' offices. Harold barks out the orders: "Get my attorney, Laurence Shaiman. Get Moses' agent, Lee Fentress, in Washington. Get Billy. Get Malone. Let's meet in New York, right now."

Having never even breathed in the outside air of Nevada, Harold is turning around and getting the next flight East. In a marathon, all-night session in a New York hotel, Moses Malone is persuaded to sign a contract with the 76ers.

For six years.

For $13.2 million.

Our plane lands at LaGuardia and I call home and get the news. I tell Doc. His mouth falls open. My initial reaction is to feel left out. After helping orchestrate dozens of deals, I am out of the country when two of the team's biggest transactions are negotiated. But then the ramifications of acquiring Moses sink in, and Doc and I both feel a little like lottery winners. The best center in basketball is now a 76er.

Well, not quite.

Moses' employer, the Houston Rockets, is not about to give up

144

without a whimper. The Rockets' attorneys scrutinize the Sixers' contract with Moses and lodge objections to some of the incentive clauses. They demand arbitration. Under the terms of free agency, they have 15 days to match the Sixers' offer. Just to further complicate everything, the Rockets' franchise is in the process of being sold. Harold Katz flies to Paris for a business meeting, and as the Rockets' sale nears completion, flies right back to New York to meet with attorneys representing present owner and prospective owner. Houston says it wants Caldwell Jones *and* Cleveland's first-round pick in the 1983 draft, the pick which we had been hoarding since the Terry Furlow deal in 1977.

That is highly unpalatable. Caldwell Jones is like owning a piece of the rock. You know he's going to be there, game after game, grabbing rebounds, playing tough defense, scoring when you need it. He is proven and he is remarkably durable. CJ is the guy you want up against your back in a foxhole. And that No. 1 pick from Cleveland, as everyone knows, could very well turn out to be 7-4 Ralph Sampson, who is being compared to Kareem and Wilt and Bill Russell.

Houston's requested arbitration occurs in New York. The federal mediator is Kingman Brewster, former president of Yale. He listens to arguments from both sides and promises a decision within ten days. Meanwhile Harold Katz, with Shaiman, flies to Houston to meet with the Rockets' new owner, Charles Thomas, another man of immense wealth. Thomas remains adamant. He wants Caldwell Jones plus the No. 1 pick.

Billy Cunningham was understandably thrilled at the prospect of having Moses Malone, but he was also distraught at the prospect of losing Caldwell Jones, the kind of player every coach covets. Too, Cleveland had been so bad for so long, that if they finished with the worst record in the East, certainly a distinct probability, then, with their pick, the Sixers would need only to win a coin flip with the team finishing with the worst record in the West, and they would have the very first pick in the 1983 draft. Well, hello there, Ralph Sampson.

Billy and I suggested that we wait Houston out. Maybe they

can't match our offer, and we keep Caldwell and the Cleveland pick, and get Moses, too.

So the agonizing and the hand-wringing continued. Finally Harold Katz said: "Look, Moses Malone is a sure thing. We know what he can do. But there is absolutely no guarantee that we can even get Ralph Sampson. First off, Cleveland has to finish last. What if they don't? What if, say, Indiana has a worse record? And even if Cleveland does finish last, then we still have to win the coin flip. As best I figure this, we've got a one-in-three shot at getting Sampson. I'm a gambler, but I don't like those odds. And I *really* don't like them when I know we can get Moses."

The deal is closed.

As it turns out, the scenario Harold Katz suggested is precisely what did occur. Cleveland did have a woeful year, winning only 23 games. But Indiana, just as Katz had astonishingly predicted, won only 20. So the draft pick we had from Cleveland wouldn't even have bought us a ticket in the Sampson sweepstakes. We wouldn't have gotten as far as the coin flip.

And, of course, we wouldn't have gotten Moses Malone, either.

But back there in the late summer of 1982, no one knew any of this would happen. Harold knew the public would really squawk about the Sixers' relinquishing their chance to pick up Ralph Sampson, and the howls could really be loud in view of Darryl Dawkins' departure and the ticket price increases. So Harold told us all: "I'll take full public responsibility if you want. I'm willing to take all the raps."

I said: "No way. We go out united."

So Moses is a Sixer. King Kong in sneakers.

Except that one of Moses' best friends is Caldwell Jones, and when Moses learns of the terms of the deal, he is crushed. He is shaken to the point that now he isn't sure he wants this to happen. King Kong is edging toward the exit before we've even got him to the top of the Empire State Building.

Harold goes one-on-one with Moses and points out the blunt bottom line: "Moses, where would you rather be? In Houston, with a losing team? Or here with a shot at the championship? We simply cannot get you without giving up CJ."

Moses desperately wanted the only thing missing in his life—an NBA title. Also, he wanted out of Houston because he had come to feel unappreciated and taken for granted. Too, he was stuck on a team that offered no supporting talent at all. Moses had to be superhuman every night and even then the Rockets struggled to win as many as they lost. With the Sixers, he knew he would have help.

And in Philadelphia, he discovered that very night, he most definitely would not go unappreciated. After his fears had been allayed, we all walked to a conference room for his introductory press conference. The Phillies were playing that night, and some of the early arrivals spotted Moses as he walked down the Veterans Stadium concourse. They chanted his name, an impromptu chorus of adulation, and later Moses would remark that was more response than he had encountered in all his seasons in Houston.

He hadn't seen anything yet . . .

10

The Odd Couple Plus One

Buzzard's Luck: Can't kill anything, and can't find something already dead . . . .

If ever an owner of a professional sports franchise was stricken with buzzard's luck, it was Irv Kosloff, the gentle, unassuming man who numbered among his possessions of 1972-73 the Philadelphia 76ers, certifiably the alltime champions of futility.

The Sixers began that season by losing their first 15 games.

And then things really got bad.

They fashioned another losing streak of 20 in a row. In all, they set a record for the most defeats in the history of the league: 73. They set another record for fewest victories in a season: 9. They set still another record for the worst won-loss percentage ever: .110.

They were a team that was light years away from even mediocrity. And every time Irv Kosloff looked up, the buzzards were circling again, cackling their cruel one-liners, like:

Kos's luck is running so bad that he stood on the beach and the tide refused to come in . . . .

Or, Kos is like the man with lockjaw and seasickness at the same time . . . .

Or, they just uprooted a tree in Israel in Kos's honor . . . .

Or, Kos is even getting hate mail from Quakers . . . .

Or, Kos's artificial flower just died . . . .

And yet through that interminable, abysmal winter, Irv Kosloff persevered admirably. He endured the sort of trauma and travail no other NBA owner had ever experienced, or has since, and he survived with remarkable patience. He did not hide out; he continued to come to every game. He delivered no public tirades. He did not chastize the players. He did not threaten to sell the team. It was a graphic demonstration of resiliency and forbearance, and it is doubtful that we will ever see its like again.

Because, you see, the owners of professional sports franchises generally have three things in common:

1. Wealth
2. Ego
3. Unpredictability

The wealth is what enables them to buy a team to begin with, and there are no more bargain basement teams out there anymore, no half-off sales. Even for the ultrawealthy, purchasing a professional team is no longer a casual whim, an impromptu indulgence.

The ego is what prompts most of them to become owners these days. A pro team is regarded as another toy, expensive, but unique. The ocean, after all, is filled with yachts, and the land teems with polo ponies, but there are only a limited number of sports teams around, and this exclusivity is part of the allure. Too, on the playing fields of the cocktail party circuit there can be no more devastating piece of oneupmanship than such a nonchalant boast as: "Oh, yes, Julius Erving works for *me*." Or, "Well, as *I* was telling Moses Malone in the locker room the other day . . . ."

The unpredictability is what furnishes the drive that generates the wealth that triggers the ego. Owners, as a rule, are impatient people. They are accustomed to quick success and instant gratification. They are demanding and opinionated, and they are used to getting their own way. So it is difficult for them to understand why their team cannot win every single game. Disap-

150

pointment is foreign to them. Failure is for others.

But when you own a sports team, you find out all about disappointment and failure. Especially you find out about them if you happen to own the 76ers.

In my tenure as general manager here, the Sixers have had three owners, each intriguing in his own way, but each disparate, polar opposites in style and temperament. So permit me to introduce you to, one by one, in chronological order, *The Odd Couple Plus One.* It is for you to decide which is which.

KOS

His parents were born in Russia and Kos was one of four children, a product of a family of immigration, and a man who personifies the American success story. He had an early love for sports, captaining his football team at Southern High in Philly, a two-way center who played with grit and gumption that made up for his lack of size. His team won the city championship and Kos earned a football scholarship to LaSalle, where he lasted less than a month. Then, bad knees having cut short his football career, he enrolled in the Temple University Dental School. But his plans for becoming a dentist evaporated after another month ("My parents couldn't afford the golf lessons," he quipped) and he wound up, at the age of 20, working for the Container Corporation of America, a salesman on the street, for the princely sum of $50 a month. His recollection is that he quit that job, "but only before they could fire me."

At 21, nursing a fierce desire for independence, he began buying up odd lots, overages and surplus paper and selling them to printers and publishers. He was, in other words, finding a way to make a profit out of what other people regarded as discards. In November of 1932 he named his business the Roosevelt Paper Company. The name was in honor of his admiration for Franklin Delano Roosevelt. This was, remember, in the depths of Great Depression. Kos's rent was $15 a month. The business has since grown to become the largest of its kind in the world, and yet Kos has never had a personal secretary, none of the trappings of wealth and power. He dictates maybe two letters a year, preferring to conduct his business by phone or in person. He doesn't have his phone calls screened; you call him and he's likely to answer himself. He still takes obvious delight in retelling how the office girls say: "You might as well answer the phone, Mr. Kosloff; all of the calls are for you, anyway."

In 1976, Kos became chairman of the board and named his son, Ted, president. But, even after 50 years, he still conducts business the same way he did when he started: a firm believer in the personal touch, the direct contact.

Kos retained his deep love for sports and, in the 1940's, when the Warriors were formed, he became a season-ticket-holder. His attorney, Ike Richman, also was the attorney for Eddie Gottlieb, the owner of the Warriors. After the 1961-62 season, Gotty, the only owner the Warriors ever had, was facing a team payroll that was getting out of hand. He ended up selling the team, for $800,000, and it moved to San Francisco. So during the 1962-63 season, there was no pro basketball team in Philadelphia, and the fan in Kos felt the absence deeply.

In the summer of 1963, Ike Richman was contacted by Danny Biasone, who was the owner of the Syracuse Nationals. Like Gottlieb, Biasone was feeling the pinch and wanted to sell his team. Ike Richman got the bug. He wanted to own a pro hoops team. But he didn't have the money to swing it on his own, so he went to Kos and tried to interest him. But Kos's business was in the midst of a major growth period. Ike Richman kept pestering, and finally Kos told him: "Look, I'll put up the money, and you do the work. I'll bankroll it, but I just don't have enough time to devote to the team and run it the way it should be run. You handle that end of it." Ike Richman eagerly agreed. The Nationals were purchased and moved to Philadelphia in the fall of 1963. The coach was Dolph Schayes and the ingredients were there for a title team, with a roster that included Hal Greer, Larry Costello, Chet Walker, John Kerr and Dave Gambee. The next season, they traded for Wilt Chamberlain, returning him to Philly.

In December of 1965, Kos was in his home, dressing for the wedding of Albert Taxin (the owner of Bookbinders restaurant) and sneaking peeks at the TV set; his basketball team was playing in Boston that night. There, seated next to the team's bench, before the cameras, Ike Richman collapsed of a massive coronary and died. Kos was left as the sole owner, and no longer the man behind the scenes.

In 1967, Irv Kosloff's team—by then they were the Sixers—would win it all. He would own it for 13 years, selling it reluctantly in May of 1976.

Kos is a shy, uncomplicated person who has to work at being outgoing. He is not one for small talk, as suggested by his rather blunt introduction of Fitz Dixon to me that memorable day: "Pat, meet your new owner." He has had three loves in his life: his family, the Roosevelt Paper Company and the Sixers. They remain his three loves, and his routine has been unchanged for more than half a century. He is an early riser and he is still in his office by 7 every morning. He still attends the Sixers games, to the point of buying eight courtside seats every season, exulting in victory, agonizing in defeat, but always politely.

There is not the slightest touch of ostentation in him, no airs. He is kindly, a genuinely nice man. But he can also cut right through pretense and get to the heart of the matter. When I first went to work for him, he said there were only two things that matter in this business: winning and selling tickets.

"Don't get sidetracked by anything else," he said. "Otherwise, you're just spinning your wheels and you're not helping the team."

Kos and his wife, Libby, developed a very close relationship with George and Lynda McGinnis, to the point of dining together frequently and dabbling in various business ventures together. George looked upon Kos as a father figure. Given Kos's patience and humanity, it was easy to see why. But there is also in Kos a refreshing quirk, a surprising sense of humor, and in unguarded moments he will drop a philosophical question on you that is delightful. He has pondered, for example, why is it that we drive on parkways but park on driveways? And his favorite puzzlement is this: What would chairs look like if our knees bent the other way? Just when you think you've got Kos pegged, he hits you with one of those.

FITZ

Fitz Eugene Dixon, Jr., might have stepped right out of the pages of *The Great Gatsby*. He is immensely wealthy, scion of two affluent families who married and merged fortunes, and socially prominent as well.

Fitz is the great-great-grandson and heir of P.A.B. Widener, nineteenth century financier and trolley car magnate. Widener (as in Widener College) was the son of a German bricklayer. He sold mutton to the Union troops during the Civil War and then parlayed that into a vast transportation empire that at one point included 500 miles of streetcar lines in Philadelphia, Chicago, New York, Pittsburgh and Baltimore. One of his partners was William Elkins, who amassed several millions in oil and public utilities. They were two of the wealthiest tycoons in Philadelphia's Gilded Age, and a dynastic intermarriage produced even more wealth. Widener's son married Elkins' daughter and it was this unification of family fortunes which Fitz inherited.

Fitz has always lived the good life, on a 500-acre estate that includes a 60-room mansion, an indoor tennis court, a one-mile horse racetrack, lush gardens and greenhouses. The flowers alone are said to be worth $1 million. The estate also includes a private landing strip for Fitz's plane, and he travels either by that or by his yacht to his summer home in Maine and winter residence in Florida.

So he is obviously to the manor born, and yet Fitz always resisted taking the easy way out. He has chaired and sponsored scores of civic and charitable causes, especially schools and hospitals. But he has also gone beyond merely opening his checkbook. For more than 16 years he taught French and English at Episcopal Academy, and coached the squash and 120-pound football teams. To his credit, he never just laid back and contented himself with clipping coupons and throwing parties.

"Insofar as I possibly can," he said, "I try to do something for others. You get out of this life exactly what you put in. I like to be occupied. The worst thing is to be a lounge lizard. It is unfortunate that many people I know, who have a certain amount of wealth, in the first place never worked for anyone else, and in the second place do nothing. These people are to be pitied. I could name a dozen of them I pity."

Fitz never had to work a day in his life. But he did. He never succumbed to the temptation of doing nothing.

He has owned pieces of most of the professional sports teams in Philadelphia, but he always had yearned to be the proprietor of a team he could call his very own. When he purchased the Sixers, he admitted: "Frankly, I want to be something other than a minority stockholder."

Prior to his purchase of the Sixers, he had seen the team play only twice, both times playoff losses to Buffalo, and he has come to very few games since he sold the team. But for the five years he owned them, he was a fanatical follower. After some initial stiffness, he really got into the game, to the point of cursing the referees from his courtside seat. And there is no doubt in my mind he would have stayed on if he hadn't, finally, become so discouraged. Fitz likes to win.

He is a very proper, reserved, Main Line type, a man of precise habits and routine. In the office at the same time every morning, lunch, martinis before dinner, the 11 o'clock news, lights out. He carries his whole day in his vest pocket. And there is always a phone number where his secretary can reach him.

Letting his hair down does not come easily to Fitz, and yet I can remember the look of delight on his face when Darryl Dawkins called him "Shorty" and fondly patted the top of his head at a team Christmas party; and the sight of his wife, Edith, a tall, stately woman, jitterbugging with Doc. Fitz poured a lot of money into the Sixers, and a lot of himself as well. He was very giving during his tenure, but in the end he began to feel that all he was getting in return was too much heartache. We came frustratingly close to winning it all, and Fitz just couldn't take any more near-misses.

While he was the owner, Fitz would entertain lavishly in his private lounge at the Spectrum on game nights. The spreads were always elaborate, and the guest list would range from 15 to 35, and Fitz would spend hours planning the menu and the program. He held court from the same seat in that lounge every night, original paintings on the wall, amid an aura of muted elegance which was never to be fouled by tobacco fumes. Fitz was fanatical about No Smoking. During his ownership, there were at least 250 game nights of the most gracious sort of dining. But in the end, the Sixers gave Fitz more indigestion than he could stand.

Most of the time, Fitz was calm, controlled, as befits a man worth millions. But he could also flare over the most petty of matters, and his anger could produce some hysterical moments. During one of his very first games as owner, he called me from his box as soon as the National Anthem had been played, and snapped: "I hate color guards. We are never to have another one on the floor. Do you understand?"

Put that way, I certainly did. I also realized that if Fitz considered a color guard too flashy, I was going to have to curb my promotional tendencies. We reined in on our halftime promotions. If color guards were out, I felt reasonably sure mud wrestling was, too. He is a highly respected horse breeder and owner, and one of his steeds won the prestigious American Gold Cup, an international, Olympic-caliber jumping competition, and I suspected Fitz wanted the Sixers playing against a backdrop of tweed, briar pipes and sips of sherry. I did sneak in a pretzel-eating contest one game—some South Philly tag-team wrestling type wolfed down about four-dozen and Fitz called me the next day and said quietly: "Please don't do that again. Edith didn't care for that."

Fitz was capable of great and sudden emotional attachments. One of the beneficiaries of this trait was Bob Babilino, who had been a Secret Service agent and had traveled with Henry Kissinger when he was Secretary of State. Fitz made Bob his chief of security, and among his other duties he shooed away spectators who might pass in front of Fitz at Sixers games and obscure his vantage point.

This, understandably, was not met with much enthusiasm by the ticket buyers, who were made to feel part of the great unwashed.

Once Fitz got into the swing of basketball and began to develop a feel for the sport, he would lapse occasionally into his own brand of humor. In the winter of 1979, the Boston Celtics had acquired Bob McAdoo from the Knicks for *three* No. 1 draft choices, a deal made strictly between the owners, without consultation of general managers or coaches on either side. So in June of that year, Fitz came into my office, grim-faced, tight-lipped, and announced that, by himself, he had acquired McAdoo. In exchange for Julius Erving. He peered intently at me, waiting for my reaction. I turned most of the shades of the rainbow. My face must have looked like those lights that used to change color on the old jukeboxes. With admirable restraint, I managed not to blurt out something like: "You imbecile, you've ruined the team!" Mostly, I just sat there in shock. Finally, Fitz could stand it no longer. He burst into laughter, loud, cackling peals. It was all a joke. Once I had been resuscitated, I managed to find some humor there. Fitz swore me to secrecy and then pulled the same gag on Billy Cunningham. Billy almost expired on the spot. Fitz broke up again.

It wasn't always easy for him, but Fitz could be one of the boys. Or, at least, try mightily. I always regretted that I never asked him, while he was enjoying his private little joke, if he thought he had loosened up enough for us to try a color guard again.

HAROLD

Definition of a genius: A man who aims at something no one else can see . . . and hits it. Harold Katz cut the heart right out of the bullseye.

While Fitz was born into great wealth, Harold Katz, like Irv Kosloff, became a multi-millionaire by dint of his own drive and tenacity. This does not detract from Fitz, who has not allowed great wealth to be a handicap to achievement. None of the three owners of the Sixers has; each has his own unique style, but each also has a clear understanding of the responsibilities of wealth. Those of us on the outside looking in may not understand it, but being rich isn't quite as easy as it appears.

Anyway, Harold grew up in South Philly, the son of a grocer, and all of his life he wanted to be a professional basketball player. But he was too short; there is not much market for 5-10 guards. So he did the next best thing: he ended up buying his very own team.

It was not in the nature of either Kos or Fitz to impose their will on the Sixers. But Harold came in as a fanatical fan; ferocious, frenetic and furiously involved.

To survive a change of ownership requires patience and flexibility. There is a fine line between becoming subservient and remaining your own man. If you are a GM and you have been in the business for several years, you tend to feel that you know a little bit about the business. But a new owner comes in and feels as if he has all the answers, and this can be crushing to your own ego. A friend of mine in the business, Dick Vertlieb, who has been the GM in Seattle, Golden State and Indiana, and also with the Seattle Mariners baseball team, says the only way you can survive is to know the mind of your owner and how he wants to operate, and then execute his game plan. If the ground rules happen to get changed, says Dick, then you're doomed. Well, it was more than a year after Harold took over before I realized that I had never really made a total commitment to him and his new team. There had been a tension between us; we are disparate personalities and we had never really meshed. I think what changed my mind was when he stuck his neck out 18 miles in September of 1982 and said he wanted Moses Malone and was going to get him, and he would take all the consequences. I found myself making a commitment to Harold then. He had broken not my spirit but my will. As completely as he was throwing himself into the team, I could see that I should be making the same effort. Harold inherited me as GM. He has given me plenty of rein. There is no written contract between us. There never has been. But he has lived up to all his commitments.

When Harold bought the team, everyone in the city and the

league wondered who he was. There was an air of mystique about him, and Harold liked that. He still does. Part of his business strategy is to keep people off balance, wondering just who is this guy and what is he doing?

He is a driven person; by his own admission compulsive, obsessive, a workaholic. He is an acclaimed marketing genius, having parlayed the idea of a weight reduction program under one roof, Nutri/Systems Inc., into a burgeoning conglomerate, with revenues totaling $124.6 million in the last fiscal year. His own personal net worth is estimated to be at least $300 million. Harold Katz has gotten fat off the fat of the land.

He is an instinctive salesman who once took a job as a Fuller Brush salesman so he could get rid of a stutter. That will tell you all you need to know about the man's ambition and his single mindedness. Only 11 years ago, he opened his first weight control center. Today there are more than 700 of them around the country, and he is poised for international expansion.

"I developed the personality to succeed," he said, "but the drive, the ambition, that's inherent, that's always been there. I was born with that. I am definitely relentless. In fact, I'd say that's the single best word to describe me. That's what I always liked about Moses Malone, the way he rebounds. He's just relentless going after the ball. We have the same style. I'm an intense competitor. I am someone who would love to learn how to relax. That's the major obstacle in my life."

He is 46 years old, twice divorced. He made himself into a millionaire by the time he was thirty-eight. He lives in the fast lane, and he has a chauffeured limo driving him along it. He defied the league and a federal mediator to get Moses Malone. Harold Katz generally gets what he sets out to get. What others consider as hopeless, he finds intriguing. That is why, at the time he bought the Sixers, it was probably a perfect marriage. For he identified with this team and its history of frustration. He saw in it some of himself: latent talent that needed only to be goaded into success.

"If this team hadn't represented a challenge," he admitted, "I probably wouldn't have bought it. But they were always the bridesmaid, loved on the road but not at home. I came in wanting to turn that around."

He is hyper, intense, a perfectionist, and very much aware of that, very much aware of the irony that if he were not so intense he would not be where he is. He likes living on the razor's edge and, figuratively, he has come to need an adrenalin fix almost daily.

"The one major reason for my success is that I never let down," he said, "never wasted time on excuses. I could always put my goals ahead of what I would rather be doing. See, all the time I was striving for what I call 'screw-you-money.' That's being at the point where you've made enough, where you're secure enough, that you can just say to the rest of the world, 'Screw you.' But once you reach a certain level, there are obligations. You become a public figure and you have to watch even more closely how you act. Anyway, I'll work 'til I die. If I took an early retirement, I'd die early, that's all."

Like his two predecessors, Kos and Fitz, Harold Katz burned to bring a championship to Philly. He is so totally immersed in the sport that he has a court in his backyard, and last winter had a satellite dish installed in a corner of his front lawn so he could pick up telecasts of NBA and college games around the clock. It is not, in fact, unusual for him to flip on the TV at 3 in the morning and watch a game.

Harold has two main ambitions. One is to become a billionaire. He has made his own study and determined, by his reckoning, that he could become the first billionaire to accumulate that much wealth without the aid of oil income. His other ambition, equally as fierce, was to win an NBA title.

Of being a billionaire, he says: "It's no longer a matter of making more and more money. You do it right and the money follows. But now the money isn't what's really important. Money is just the way you keep score in this game."

And among owners of professional sports franchises, the way you keep score is by counting championships.

And just getting close doesn't count at all. . . .

11

Victor, Pepper and Little Arlene

HER NAME WAS Arlene Katz and her *schtick* was her appetite. She could out-eat the Fifth Fleet. You invited her over for dinner and all you had to do was pour some oil and vinegar on the lawn and let her graze. She billed herself as "Little Arlene," and to sit her down at a table was to watch the methodical destruction of most of the agricultural output of the Great Plains.

Little Arlene was first brought to my attention by Craig Raymond, a 6-11 center from Brigham Young who was playing minor league basketball in Wilkes Barre, Pennsylvania. "They had a grand opening of a hamburger stand there," he reported, still somewhat in awe, "and this woman ate about 80 cows."

Little Arlene sounded like a natural.

This was during my first time around with the 76ers, in the 1968-69 season, and I contacted Little Arlene. She was eager. We arranged an eating contest, to commence at the start of a Sixers game and to continue until everyone succumbed to indigestion. The

161

gist of the promotion was that Little Arlene would take on any five gourmands and, by herself, exceed their combined caloric intake. The menu, Little Arlene added confidently, didn't matter.

We settled on a dietician's delight: pizza, hot dogs and Coke. The opponents were five trenchermen from South Philly, a quintet of junk-food addicts, whose girth was graphic testimony to their feasting prowess. Their leader called himself the Galloping Glutton, and the circumference of his waist looked to be roughly equal to the equator. The smart money figured the mysterious Little Arlene was badly overmatched.

We were all, of course, expecting some heroically proportioned Amazon, a Brunhilde wearing a form-fitting poncho. We were most definitely not prepared for what we got. Little Arlene showed up, as scheduled, and she was, well, *little*. Tiny. Petite. Dainty. Barely five feet tall. With neither rotund belly nor tractor-trailer hips. There is the distinctly uneasy feeling that we have been had. Her opponents, the Philadelphia Phill-ups, are helpless with laughter.

And then Little Arlene delicately sits down and launches into a gastronomic orgy. By halftime, the Phill-ups are reeling away from the table, staggering around in belching agony, ricocheting off the walls on their way to the men's room. Little Arlene just sits there, eating relentlessly, dabbing at her mouth with a napkin, smiling pleasantly, and pausing only to ask, very politely: "Pass the hot dogs, please?"

It is a rout.

By the third quarter, Little Arlene is all alone. The Phill-ups have long since surrendered and stumbled away in search of stomach pumps. By now, Little Arlene has consumed 23 hot dogs, 22 large slices of pizza and 16 Cokes. She allows as how she would be willing to challenge all comers to an oyster-eating contest at Bookbinders after the game is over.

"Arlene," I sigh, "enough is enough."

Later, we get her hotel bill. The tab includes a full-course roast beef dinner, which Little Arlene had eaten *before* the contest.

Arlene's digestive tract belongs in the Smithsonian.

My guru was Bill Veeck, that marvelous, old one-legged promotional genius who knew how to put people in the stands, and, more importantly, how to keep them coming back. Bill subscribed to the old theory of Ya Gotta Have a Gimmick, especially in professional sports. We are, after all, in the entertainment business, and our competition extends far beyond other teams. One of Veeck's first mandates was this: You cannot sell a team solely on its won-loss record. That is just too risky. For a long time it was assumed that people would always support a winner. And owners who make that assumption usually end up filing for bankruptcy. Veeck's other piece of advice to me was: For every five dollars the fan plunks down for a ticket, give him six dollars' worth of entertainment.

"You're in the business of creating memories," he said. "When the fan leaves your stadium, you want him to take a pleasant memory with him. Whether your team wins or loses is beyond your control. Whether he has had a good time, in a facility that's clean, that offers the little extras, *those* things you can control."

I had had my first exposure to promotion in my junior year at Wake Forest. In mid-November of 1960, I was awakened from a sound sleep by this heavy, persistent thudding on my dorm room door. The knocker was Jerry Steele, a varsity basketball player from Elkin, North Carolina. He informed me that the Annual Varsity-Freshman basketball game was only a week away and I had been elected to promote it. That election was one I had won by default: no one else wanted the job. I wasn't exactly thrilled with it, either, since I was devoting every moment of my life at that point to becoming a major league catcher. Jerry Steele had a rich Southern drawl and a very persuasive manner, however; the fact that he was 6-8, 240 pounds, made him pretty convincing, too. In making all the arrangements, selling tickets, setting up bands and homecoming queens, in seeing all of these myriad details finally mesh and come together in a successful promotion, I was smitten by this fascinating business, although I didn't realize it at the time.

Later, when I had signed my contract with the Phillies, I managed to sneak a look at the report sent to the front office on me by the scout, Wes Livingood: "Will never make it as a big league catcher, but can in the front office."

He turned out to be quite a prophet.

My first team was the Miami Marlins, whose general manager was Bill Durney, a hearty, bluff man who lived for the moment. That summer, Bill Veeck's book, *Veeck As In Wreck*, came out, and I devoured it. Bill Durney had been Veeck's running mate in a number of his more memorable promotions, so I picked Durney's brain all summer, and then that fall drove to Veeck's estate. He was sitting on the veranda, sunning himself, his wooden leg resting on a nearby stool. Eight hours later, I left him, totally overwhelmed. He had advised me to learn how to type, acquire a working knowledge of accounting, and learn everything possible about advertising. Those, he said, were absolutely indispensable for anyone starting out in promotions. As an eager neophyte, I committed every sentence he uttered to memory, and later visited him several more times for advanced instruction.

In 1965, in Spartanburg, South Carolina, I got the chance to try out my promotional abilites as the brash, young general manager of a Class A minor league baseball club. For opening night, I hired a sky diver to tumble down in a spectacular free fall, and then parachute to the pitching mound with the first ball. The lighting at that level of sports was about one bulb removed from Thomas Edison's first invention. The sky diver looked at all those hot wires ringing the park and said he'd feel a lot safer if we would turn off the power as he made his descent; in the event of a capricious gust of wind, he didn't relish the prospect of being blown onto one of those live wires and getting fried. Fine, no problem. Except I forgot to tell the manager of the visiting team that things would get a touch dark before the game started. And so the other team's starting pitcher that evening, a young fireballer named Dick Selma, cut loose with a blazer just as the lights went dim and very nearly decapitated his catcher. The manager accused me of premeditated sabotage. The sky diver, meanwhile, came down far beyond the left field wall and ended up somewhere out in a grove of trees.

There have been more auspicious promotional debuts.

Bill Veeck was about 30 years ahead of his time. Today, of course, every franchise has some sort of promotion for every game, but back when I was starting out, promotions were frowned upon, regarded as freak shows that somehow detracted from the main event rather than adding to it. I can still remember John Quinn, the GM of the Phillies, pointing a bony finger in my eager face and saying: "You take all of your nylons and your giveaways, young man, and you give me nine good ball players, and I'll fill the park every night!"

I had not exactly endeared myself to Mr. Quinn earlier with one of my promotions at Spartanburg called a Barnyard Scramble. We rounded up every form of livestock known to man, turned them loose on the diamond, and had our players try to catch them. Pat Skrable, the Phillies' prize outfield prospect, nearly dislocated his shoulder diving for a calf in left field.

My first stint with the 76ers, we had an NBA doubleheader and I had been warned to come up with something special. Forget the barbershop quartets and the animal chases, kid. This is Philly, a big town, and the people are too sophisticated. You need a block-buster. This was the winter of 1969 and the Phillies had a talented but troubled slugger named Dick Allen. He was a great hitter but he suffered through a tempestuous relationship with the fans, who booed him mercilessly. Allen had formed a singing group and cut a record, "Echoes of November." It was about as bad as it sounds. It was on the—honest—Groovey Grooves label. At halftime of the second game of the doubleheader, Dick Allen sang "Echoes of November." Booed all summer, he got a standing ovation.

The halftime entertainment for the first game was my *piece de resistance*. His name is Victor and he goes about eight feet and 600 pounds. He is a bear. But not your run-of-the-mill Yosemite Park scavenger. Victor has a special talent.

He wrestles.

Victor has been declawed and muzzled so that the carnage can be kept to an acceptable minimum. He is, of course, unbeatable. By a human, anyway. But there is no problem in getting volunteers down from the stands. Some try to out-quick Victor, diving for one of his legs and yanking. They might as well be trying to pull down a building. Victor does not budge easily. Usually he puts a conclusive end to every match by simply sitting on his opponent. Victor is actually a mild-mannered animal, as bears go. This is good. If Victor ever regarded this as anything but fun, we could have had some serious problems. Anyway, nobody lasts even 30 seconds against Victor, but the crowd loves every minute of it, especially when he sits on his haunches and sucks down a bottle of soda.

Every place I go after that—Chicago, Atlanta, back to Philadelphia—Victor the wrestling bear is a promotional staple. He makes the rounds with me. In Chicago, however, the anticruelty society says it will not allow Victor to wrestle during the halftime of one of the Bulls' games unless they can approve each of his opponents. I can't see that there is any question here; the last thing Victor needs is protection. I mean, who can hurt a *bear?* Dutifully, we draft opponents for Victor out of our own office. I even end up going a round with him; well, one-tenth of a round, maybe. I've often thought later how proud my mother must have been to see her son on TV, being ingloriously pinned to the mat by a fullgrown bear.

From Chicago, I go to Atlanta as general manager of the Hawks, and I roll in all of the old standbys, and then I hear for the first time of a trained pig act called "Uncle Heavy and His Porkchop Revue." Personally, I had always thought pigs were hopelessly dumb and beyond training. Wrong, Bacon Breath. Uncle Heavy's porkers can sit up on command, whiz down slides, do most of the tricks you see wild animals perform in a circus. I thought the Porkchop Revue was a stunning success. But the next day, John Wilcox, the owner-appointed overseer of the Hawks, a moneyed type who was accustomed to the country club life, curtly informed me that he had never been so embarrassed, nor the club more humiliated. The only good pig, he said rather forcefully, was one that was turned slowly on a spit and basted with barbecue sauce. I thought that was a narrowminded viewpoint but, having become fond of collecting a steady paycheck, I assured him Uncle Heavy would not be invited back.

But the next year, in 1974, having just rejoined the 76ers, I got a call from a gentleman who said he had a surefire halftime show for me: "The Ham 'n Egg Revue." It included, among other things, a trained chicken and a pig that could sing. Specifically, Pepper the Singing Pig. This was too good to pass up. The latent pig fancier in me was hopelessly hooked. Now normally you can't get the media interested in your promotions. But, for some reason, the Philly press latched onto the idea of Pepper and fell in love with him. Or her. We were never sure. Every day there is a story about Pepper coming to the Spectrum. The problem is that while interest is created, which is precisely what you want, expectations also were built. Finally, they were built too high.

The fans were expecting the second coming of Enrico Caruso by now.

Pepper falls a good number of high C's short of that.

Probably we should have auditioned Pepper. It turns out that the handler kneels next to the pig, holds a microphone in front of its snout, then reaches around in a friendly hug with the other arm and proceeds to punch the pig in the ribs. Pepper, of course, responds with assorted squeals and grunts of protest. It requires considerable imagination to even faintly interpret this as any form of singing. To make matters worse, during the course of Pepper's concert, one of the other pigs decides to relieve itself on the Spectrum floor. This act is interpreted as a critical judgment of Pepper's singing. The crowd agrees with the other pig and relieves itself of thunderous boos. We can't give Pepper the hook fast enough. It is a certified disaster. The next day's headlines read:

76ERS LOSE TO KNICKS; PIGS BOOED
WILLIAMS HAS HIS OWN
BAY OF PIGS FIASCO

The whole idea behind promotions is to lure the people into your building, and once you've got them there, keep them entertained. The 76ers have gone to some bizarre lengths to do that.

Promotions have been as varied as mud wrestling and God and Country Night and Salute to Israel. (There has been only an occasional demand for equal time from those requesting a Sodom and Gomorrah Night.) The Sixers have offered free tickets to anyone taller than Tom Burleson (7-3 center) or shorter than Calvin Murphy (5-9 guard) or with larger feet than Bob Lanier (18½-EEE).

There was also Blind Date Night. On Valentine's Day, of course. A section of the Spectrum was set off for those wishing to capitalize. Men were sold odd-numbered seats, women even-numbered. Forty-four men showed up; one woman. She observed that those were rather frightening odds.

One of the keys to promotions is spontaneity and timeliness. You start doing things, and things have a way of happening.

In mid-January of 1983, for example, the Sixers and the Milwaukee Bucks played one of those down-to-the-wire, bite-your-fingernails-back-to-your-elbow games that was won by the Sixers, 122-121, when Marc Iavaroni sank two free throws with only five seconds left in the game. The referee alleged that Iavaroni had been fouled by the Bucks' Marques Johnson in a loose ball scramble. Don Nelson, the Milwaukee coach, was so incensed at the call that he charged out onto the court, and in a Gypsy Rose Lee impromptu strip of outrage, began peeling off his clothes. He ripped off his sportcoat so violently that he split it halfway up the back. Then he wound up and flung the coat in a glorious arc. Like a fluttering helicopter, it landed on the court. Nelson, of course, was ejected. In his pique, he never bothered to retrieve his coat.

The Sixers kept it. Don Nelson said they could have it. Which, of course, gave birth to the halftime promotion for the next Milwaukee visit: a sportcoat-throwing contest with Nellie's tattered jacket. The league office said: No-no. But the Bucks said: Why not? And Don Nelson, a former player and, thankfully for the Sixers, a consummate good sport, said: "Hey, we're in the entertainment business. If that's fun, go to it. I will not, however, be a participant." The league office lifted its embargo. The coat-throwing contest went on as scheduled. And the Sixers nipped the Bucks in overtime, 104-101. Don Nelson buttoned and unbottoned his coat several times in those anxious moments, but he made certain he didn't remove it.

One thing about promotions is that you never quite know where your next one is coming from . . . and sometimes you never know when a winner is staring you right in the face. During the 1974-75 season, the Sixers had a Halloween promotion, which was occupying all of my time that particular night. So I gave short shrift to Barry Abrams, who is in the record business and also worked on our statistical crew, when he came up to me that night with this skinny kid who was introduced as a singer. The kid was desperately clinging to this tape; it was a record he had cut and he was pleading with us to allow him to play it over the PA before the game. Barry Abrams kept telling me: "This is going to be a biggie. You really ought to hear this kid sing." And I'm brushing him off impatiently, with: "Yeah, yeah, sure, Barry. Look, go up there to the sound booth and ask the electricians if it's okay with them." Dutifully, Abrams and the skinny kid go running up to the rafters. They may have bribed the electricians, for all I know. Anyway, the song comes on and I have a vague recollection of three women politely applauding when the tape is over. To my considerable chagrin, that same song, *Mandy*, becomes No. 1 on the charts, and the skinny kid, Barry Manilow, never has to plead with electricians ever again.

One of my favorite promotions was Paul Anderson, the weightlifter who was billed as the world's strongest man. Paul could benchpress most of downtown Philadelphia. At halftime, we would bring down the eight heaviest men we could find in the audience and they would get up on a table, four to each side, and Paul would squat down under the table, position it on his shoulders, and stand up. But one game in Atlanta, we hit the Fat Farm jackpot. The eight people who waddled down out of the stands all were 400-plus-pounders. The problem was, they were so gargantuan only four of them could fit on the table. Paul lifted them. Effortlessly. I was the one who had the difficult part: I had to tell those other four elephants there was no room for them. I did it from a considerable distance.

In Chicago, in 1969, we came up with a mascot called Benny the Bull. He was portrayed by a young real estate salesman and he was an immediate hit. Benny the Bull was one of the earliest, if not the very first, of the critter mascots which now proliferate in every stadium, arena and ballpark. The most famous of these is the San Diego Chicken, and probably the second most successful is the Phillie Phanatic, who was invented for the Phillies in 1976 by Bonnie Erickson and Wayde Harrison. A year later, those two created Big Shot for the 76ers. Following the Phanatic was almost impossible, and Big Shot's fortunes weren't helped along by Lou Scheinfeld's public charge that he smelled. We thought that maybe Big Shot might have more appeal if he had an accomplice, so in 1981 Harrison-Erickson came up with a companion, a fuzzy yellow creature called Hoops. We auditioned half of the Delaware Valley for the part of Hoops, but it still wasn't catching on.

Finally, succumbing to impatience and a lack of better judgment, I put on the Hoops costume in a desperate attempt to prove that he really could be sold. This was during a Sixers-Seattle game in January 1982 at the Spectrum. I didn't have contact lenses at the time and there's no room for glasses inside the Hoops outfit, so I was going at this blind. But an amazing transformation takes place when you put on one of those costumes. Maybe it's the guaranteed anonymity, but the most mild-mannered of people become suddenly brazen and adolescent once inside a mascot costume. You feel slightly giddy and your inhibitions magically melt away. It's a little like the drunk putting on a lampshade at a party. And you can get away with behavior that, on the street, would get you arrested.

Anyway, Seattle has called a timeout and here I am playing the role of Hoops, and I find myself slithering along on the floor on my fuzzy yellow belly, creeping into the middle of the Seattle huddle. The coach, Lenny Wilkens, is in the midst of a tactical discussion and he looks up to see this creature sneaking in to listen. Now I am absolutely no threat to steal any top secrets, but Wilkens comes charging at me, swinging his clipboard and kicking. I make a hasty and ignominious retreat. The upshot of all this is that Hoops is gradually phased out. The Sixers still have Big Shot, that portly, blue frizzy thing with oversized sunglasses who dunks the ball, with the aid of a small trampoline, and then gives the ball away to somebody in the audience.

Two of the other promotional staples at Sixers' games are half-time shooting contests, in which anyone who can sink a basket from mid-court wins a trip to some exotic place like Hawaii, and the playing of the National Anthem by Grover Washington, Jr. Grover doesn't play before every game, only the biggies, and most of the playoffs. He is an internationally acclaimed jazz saxophonist, and he is also a basketball fanatic and a 76ers season-ticket-holder. Doc and Grover have formed a mutual admiration society, each intrigued by the other's artistry and improvisationm Grover, in fact, composed a piece which he has dedicated to Julius Erving. And Doc stands there before a game, if Grover is playing, totally absorbed and enraptured. It is, when you think about it, a natural pairing, a musician and an aerialist, each a grand master in his field.

The 76ers have, for many years now, possessed a couple of natural, built-in promotions. One is named Dave Zinkoff and the other is Harvey Pollack.

Dave Zinkoff is known to one and all as The Zink. With a handle like that, he should be a disc jockey, and it is, of course, his voice which is so familiar wherever basketball is played, a distinctive hybrid somewhere between a stentorian delivery of a Shakespearean monologue and gravel being swished around the bottom of a bucket.

Zink was born on May 15, 1910, in Kiev, Russia. At the age of one, he was brought to the U.S. by his parents, Jews who were fleeing persecution. He went to Central High in Philadelphia, then graduated from Temple. His folks operated a deli in West Philly (Dagwood sandwiches a specialty) and in 1935 a man named Red Rosan introduced The Zink to Eddie Gottlieb, who at that time owned a professional basketball team called the Philadelphia SPAHS. The team was going bigtime, playing its home games at the Broadwood Hotel, and Gotty, in search of some class, decided he

171

needed an announcer to work the public address system. Gotty heard two sentences from this short, feisty little banty rooster and knew he had his voice. Zink, though, drove a hard bargain: $5 for every Saturday night game, *plus* Gotty had to pick Zink up at the deli and drive him to the games. Through Gotty, Zink met Abe Saperstein, the owner of the Harlem Globetrotters, and Zink traveled the world with them, enhancing their routines with his nonstop banter over the microphone. Other than the 1981-82 season, when the new regime temporarily retired him, Zink has always been the voice of the Sixers, tossing out *bon mots* in that style that is imitated in every playground along the East Coast.

When Dave Zinkoff intones: "Two minutes left in this ball game," the hairs on the nape of your neck stand at attention. He has a flair for the theatrical; indeed, The Zink would be the logical choice to do the play-by-play whenever Armageddon rolls around.

His favorite spiel is reading off the license plate of someone who has parked illegally in the Spectrum lot. Most transgressors blithely ignore warnings to move, but Zink can have them out of their seats and running frantically when he says: "The owner of a red Ford with Pennsylvania plates ENG 462, your lights are on, your doors are locked . . . and your engine is running!"

Over the years, Zink has searched for new ways to credit players with baskets, and he has come up with Gola goal, Two for Shue, a pair for Share (Chuck Share was a 7-foot center with St. Louis), Dipper Dunk (Wilt, of course), Kerr-plunk (pivotman John Kerr), a gem from Clem (Clemon Johnson). Lately he added Malone . . . alone. Probably his best was when World B. Free was with the Sixers and would sink one of those long rainbow jumpers and Zink would keen shrilly: "F-r-e-e-e-e-e-e-e-e-e-e-e-!" And there is his pregame introduction of Doc, in which he mumbles at the beginning, running the words together, low and fast, and then builds to a crescendo that gets the crowd wailing: "At the other forward, fromtheUniversityofMassachusettsNumber6Julius . . . . Er-r-r-r-r-r-r-r-r-r-rving!"

People have a hard time sitting on their hands when The Zink has a mike in his.

As for Harvey Pollack, he is a computer who happened to be born a human. They call him "Super Stat." He is the marvel of minutiae, the sultan of statistics. Harvey was born five blocks from old Connie Mack Stadium and grew up watching baseball games for free simply by falling in at the back of the line of every kid's group that was parading into the left field bleachers seats. Scouts, CYO outings, Harvey always managed to finagle his way into the park. He went to Temple and as manager of the basketball team fell in love with stats, and sports. He served in the Army and when he came out worked as a sportswriter for the *Philadelphia Bulletin*, for $28 a week. That was from 1945 to 1949. He was also keeping the stats for local colleges and Gotty hired him to be the Warriors' stat man as well.

That was in 1946, and the Warriors proceeded to win the NBA title that season. Harvey has been with Philadelphia ever since, even while working for *TV Guide* and for the city recreation department. Harvey's Sixers Yearbook is annually one of the most sought-after of publications. It is the NBA fan's bible, a treasure trove of the statistically bizarre and esoteric. If a number can be attached to a feat, Harvey will find a way to do it. He can tell you what happened and project, numerically, what is likely to happen. He is the Pharaoh of Phigures.

So the Sixers have The Zink's voice as a built-in promotion and they have Harvey Pollack to push the right buttons and dispense the news, but there is one more personality to be dealt with, and he does not fit into any convenient category for labeling. His name is Al Domenico, and for the better part of two decades he has been the Sixers' trainer.

Al is a character out of Damon Runyan. He grew up in Northeast Philly, was a medic in the Marines and started as a trainer with Roller Derby and wrasslin'. When he is not wrapping ankles and generally ministering to the infirm of the team, his favorite haunts are the racetrack and the golf course. Among his other attributes, Al is one of the NBA's premier bench jockeys, possessor of an acerbic wit and an acid tongue. More than one even-tempered player has stormed to the Sixers' bench contemplating homicide over Al's relentless ridicule. This, of course, works to the Sixers' advantage because the player cannot see clearly through the mist of rage blurring his eyes, and while he is fantasizing about throttling his tormentor, his mind is not on basketball and he becomes an easy mark. Between his barbs at players and his equally vitriolic assault on referees, it is safe to assume that Al has won some games for the Sixers, as surely as he has pulled out others by making the hurt ambulatory.

They called Bill Veeck "Barnum Bill," in homage of and reference to another pretty fair showman. In terms of promotion, Veeck's mind was a stiletto among butter knives. Of his amputated leg, Veeck once said that a man with a wooden leg is automatically colorful. Long John Silver, he suggested, would hardly have become an immortal character in fiction if he had been nothing more than a handsome bloke who went about killing people. The peg leg helped a whole lot. And that's sort of the philosophy of promotions. Your team, after all, isn't going to win every night.

If it's clean, legal and moral, then do it . . . and you never know how long the repercussions may last. A Sixers' season-ticket-holder, for example, said he was in Miami a while back having a cup of coffee at a counter, and he fell into casual conversation with a small woman on the next stool. He happened to start talking sports, specifically the 76ers, and the woman brightened perceptibly. She rummaged through her purse and pulled out this faded, yellowed newspaper clipping. It was an account of a Sixers game, at which a woman had defeated five men in an eating contest.

"I'm Arlene Katz," said the woman, introducing herself. And then she pointed at that faded clipping and said excitedly: "That's me in that story. I'm Little Arlene."

12

For $13 Million, He Ought To Be Named Moses

ON THE SURFACE, there is absolutely nothing to suggest that Moses Eugene Malone is the best player in basketball. He is not the biggest player in the league. There are better bodies. There are bigger hands. There are higher leapers. There are faster runners. There are more accurate shooters.

Oh, Moses is not exactly small nor helpless, not at 6-10, 255 pounds. But there are a dozen centers in the NBA who are taller, a few by almost half a foot. He is a quick jumper but his vertical leap will stagger no one. And his hands are inordinately small for a man of his size. And he won't win many foot races.

So what is it that makes him so special?

"Moses is a freak of nature," said Dr. Michael Clancy, the Sixers' team physician. "There's just no other way to explain it. He can't jump. He doesn't run well. Bad hands. But he doesn't ever run down. He doesn't ever quit trying. And the rougher it gets, the better he plays. It's like he thrives on the banging and the contact. He plays his best when there are three people hanging all over him. I swear there are times when he goes out of his way to get bumped."

He does, indeed, seem to feed on the energy radiated by those trying to contain him. And his stamina has become legendary. The longer the game goes, the stronger Moses becomes. If the NBA lengthened its games to five quarters, the 76ers might never lose. If they played six quarters, everyone else would be horizontal and Moses would be out there playing by himself.

But for all of his individual success, Moses had never played on a championship team, and there were whispers that he could never fit in with a team that likes to run, that he had to play a deliberate, slow-down style in which the offense always revolved around him, and that he played almost no defense, preferring to hoard all of his energy for scoring and rebounding.

It would turn out that none of these criticisms was valid. But the point is, at the time that Harold Katz spent $13.2 million to acquire Moses Malone, it was a considerable gamble.

There are no guarantees in life, let alone sports. A lot of millionaires have spent sizable chunks of cash on promising horseflesh, then have seen their dreams of becoming owners of a Triple Crown shattered. Their colt comes up lame. Or doesn't like the starting gate. Or spooks easily. Or has no interest at all in running.

But what had sold Harold on Moses was Moses' attitude. They had talked for hours and hours, and Moses never mentioned money. All he had talked about was his desire to win a championship, to do whatever it would take. Harold is adept at sizing up people, and he was convinced that Moses was genuine, sincere . . . and worth the money.

In retrospect, of course, Moses now looks like a bargain, even at $13 million. But at the time, Harold was shooting some very large dice.

"The reason I think I have been a success in business," he said, "is that I have never been afraid to squeeze the trigger."

So he had squeezed the trigger and bagged Moses, but it would be nine months before we would know whether he had squeezed off a very large and very expensive blank, or whether he had cut the heart out of the bull's eye.

We knew that Moses' credentials were gilt-edged in Houston. But could he duplicate them in Philadelphia? He had led the league in scoring and in rebounding, twice had been the Most Valuable Player, and he had averaged playing 42 of a possible 48 minutes, night after night after night. But how would he fare with a different team, in new surroundings?

He was introduced to the literati in Philadelphia at a chaotic press conference on the night of September 15, 1982. Frankly, there was some concern about how he would handle himself. His relations with the media during his stay in Houston had been strained, at best.

Not to worry. Moses said all the right things. He paid proper homage to Julius Erving. He wore jeans and a plain brown shirt, and in that sweaty, noisy gathering he spoke in a low, rumbling voice. Neither his words nor his wardrobe glittered falsely. "It's Doc's show, and I just want to watch the show," he began. "In the ABA, Doc was always a great show, and now I've got a chance to play with Doc and I think it's gonna be a better show. My situation will be different than when they got George McGinnis. George and Doc were both forwards. I know what I've got to do to help this team. I'm not gonna try to do what I can't do. I'm just gonna play my game—attack the boards, go to the offensive boards, look for the fast break, look to rebound. I came into the league right from high school, a kid just like Darryl Dawkins. They tried to put labels on me. Can't do this, can't do that. Basically, I can do anything in the world with the ball."

Moses had not been scripted for this. It was all impromptu. He said he felt relieved coming to Philadelphia because now he would be surrounded by a strong supporting cast and wouldn't be expected to carry an entire team every game. I remember taking him to the Phillies' locker room after his press conference; they were playing the Cardinals that night. Pete Rose made a big fuss over him, and Louis Aguayo, who is 5-9, couldn't get over how big Moses was, and he kept asking Moses to hold out his arm so he could

177

walk under it. Moses was equally delighted by the attention and the reception.

In the euphoria over his arrival, however, there was also a somber note. The Sixers were going to have to cut loose Steve Mix to make room for all their youngsters. Billy Cunningham had been almost unwilling to play Steve the last two playoffs simply because he didn't match up well with the opposition. Also, there was a major financial consideration: Steve's contract was up, and it called for $225,000 a year. Moses' salary and the fact that Steve, at 35, was by now a spot player, made him expendable.

Steve Mix always had been an amazing worker. His staying power was legendary. Other than Kareem Abdul-Jabbar, he was the only NBA player still left from the 1969 draft. In fact, Steve, Kareem and Elvin Hayes, who had been drafted in 1968, were the only players still in the NBA who had been collegians in the 1960's. The Sixers needed recycling at this point, however. Milwaukee did tender Steve an offer sheet and the Sixers had 15 days to match that or let him go.

Steve had been drafted out of Toledo by the Detroit Pistons. He was a fifth-round pick at a time when there were only 14 teams in the League. He was a bench forward for Detroit for two seasons, and then he was waived prior to the 1971 training camp. He took a job loading trucks at a warehouse and played minor league basketball. After that season, he finagled tryouts with four different NBA teams, including the Sixers. He was reasonably confident of making that 1972-73 Sixers team, for it was the one that would compile that inglorious 9-73 record that very season. Incredibly, Steve Mix did not make that team. Most players would have just given up at that point. I mean, when the team with the worst record ever cuts you, that is the ultimate rejection. There is not an ounce of give-up in Steve, however. And there is a whole lot of want-to in him. He comes back and tries out again the next year, and this time he makes the Sixers. He has some big scoring nights. The following season, 1974-75, he even makes the All-Star team. It is one of the more implausible success stories. Rejected by the most futile team ever, two years later he is an All-Star. He is wired tight, an intense, aggressive competitor who plays belligerently. He has no speed, no quickness, and he only has two basic offensive moves and everyone in the NBA knows them by heart. And they still can't stop him. He either backs in and then sweeps up a little lefthanded push-hook, or he shoots a turnaround jumper from out on the wing, an area of the court which he names "Mixville." With the arrival of Julius Erving in 1976, of course, Steve becomes a nonstarter. But there were a lot of winters when it was comforting to see him come in off the bench. Steve never suffered in silence; if he had a problem, the whole world knew about it. But he lasted nine seasons with the Sixers, and every year the team would go into the draft and pick a couple of promising young forwards and every year they would go to camp and get beat out by Steve Mix, who would shove them aside just as though he were still on the loading platform of that warehouse.

The Sixers finally decided not to match Milwaukee's offer and Steve ended up with the Bucks and milked most of the 1982-83 season out of them. He finally was cut, but, amazingly, was picked up by the Los Angeles Lakers just in time for the '83 playoffs. Steve Mix is more resilient than a rubber band, and he has an incredible knack for landing on his feet.

One other veteran with a hefty salary became expendable prior to the opening of camp in the fall of 1982: Lionel Hollins. He was 29, coming off injuries, and the team payroll needed pruning to accommodate Moses Malone's $2 million a year paycheck. Plus, we needed to provide more playing time for Clint Richardson and Franklin Edwards. Just before the season started, the Sixers shipped Lionel to San Diego for their fourth-round pick in 1983 and second rounder in 1984, and the Clippers also assumed most of his salary. The Sixers kept their top four rookies: Marc Iavaroni, Mark Mc-Namara, Russ Schoene and Mitchell Anderson. That, too, was with an eye to the payroll. We knew that down the road we would need veteran help, but in September none is available. We thought we had signed Bob McAdoo, but at the last minute he had changed his mind and decided to sign with the Lakers.

Everything looks promising, but on the very first day of camp

179

there is one rather prominent absentee.

Maurice Cheeks.

Mo is unhappy with his contract, which still has four years to go. His attorney, Lance Luchnick, had been making ominous noises all summer, but we had assumed Mo would be in camp regardless. I finally tracked Mo down in Chicago and persuaded him to fly to Philadelphia to meet with Harold Katz and myself. He agreed. The problem was that the same night Mo flew in, Harold was being honored at a black tie dinner in the Bellevue Stratford Hotel in Center City. We wanted to keep the negotiations quiet so we ended up with some rather bizarre cloak-and-dagger antics. I took Mo to the hotel and then, trying to find a hiding place, parked him on the window ledge out in front of the hotel, where a couple of big potted trees concealed him. Mo sits there for the better part of an hour. The banquet finally ends and Harold comes out, in his tux. We find an empty conference room. Mo, it turns out, is mostly concerned with his longterm future. He wants to continue playing for the Sixers, but he wants a guarantee that he'll be here for a long time. We agree to an extension of his contract. Mo reports to camp the next day and responds with the best season of his career, including his first selection to the All-Star team. It also must have been the only time in the history of negotiations that a hotel window ledge was used as a waiting room.

Training camp at Lancaster goes smoothly. There is an addition to the staff, a young man named John Kilbourne, a dancer who has studied with prima ballerinas, choreographed his own shows and made movies. He knows all about anatomy and flexibility. Matty Goukas had encountered him during the LA summer league and was intrigued with his theories about preventing muscle pulls by doing exercises that keep a body lithe and supple. John had done some work in this area for Larry Brown, when Larry coached at UCLA. John was invited to the Sixers' camp, and made such an impact and was so well received by the players that he joined the team on a fulltime basis. He obviously contributed because the team was relatively injury-free through almost the entire regular season.

That 1982-83 season begins for the Sixers in Madison Square Garden. I ride up in Harold's limo with the owner, John Nash and Dr. Norm Horvitz, who is the medical director of Harold's Nutri/Systems, Inc. Tip-off is scheduled for 7:30, but the traffic in the Lincoln Tunnel is backed up in a clogged snarl. By the time we arrive at the Garden, it's already 7:10 P.M. No time for a leisurely gourmet meal. Instead, we dash into a McDonald's across the street, stand in line with the winos, muggers and other New York people of the night, and rush back to the Garden carrying bags of burgers and fries. We wolf down the food while Moses and the Sixers inhale the Knicks. Heartburn is a small price to pay for such a debut.

The Sixers open at home the very next night, against the New Jersey Nets, who have none other than Darryl Dawkins at center. Moses plays well and so does Darryl, obviously relishing the role of the prodigal son making his return. But the Sixers break open the game in the final five minutes and win going away. Moses seizes every rebound down the stretch. A packed Spectrum accords him a lusty ovation.

Any lingering questions about Moses are emphatically answered early in the season. The hated Celtics come in, and the Sixers prevail in *double overtime.* Moses plays 56 of the 58 minutes. It is clear that this is not just another overpaid superstar content to collect his check.

Philadephia is unique in that it already is home to five of the most famous names in professional sports, all of whom are set apart by their effort. They are Pete Rose, Steve Carlton, Mike Schmidt, Bobby Clarke and Julius Erving. And what sets them apart, besides their obvious talents, is their desire and their consistency and their singlemindedness of purpose. You never see any of them give less than his best. To this list, a sixth name can now be added: Moses Malone.

When the Sixers first acquired Moses, Coach Pat Riley of LA said: "The Sixers just got their missing link." It seemed, almost immediately, to be an accurate prophecy.

Moses had gone directly from Petersburg, Virginia, High

School into the ABA. He had suffered a broken foot during the 1975-76 season, which is when the ABA folded. His contract at that time was $300,000 a year, which was enormous back then. Portland took Moses in the ABA dispersal draft. But the Blazers find a healthy Bill Walton in camp that year, and Moses looks lost, unsure of himself. Portland wants to move Moses and they call everywhere, including Philly. Yes, that's right. The Sixers had a chance to acquire Moses six years before they did. But they had also just committed $1 million to Caldwell Jones, another million to Darryl Dawkins, and several millions to George McGinnis and Julius Erving. The last thing the Sixers felt they needed at that point was another huge contract, to a player coming off an injury besides. Also, remember that at that point Moses had not established himself as the monster in the middle that he would become. This is one rather spectacular case when hindsight would have proven invaluable.

Anyway, Buffalo takes Moses off Portland's anxious hands, for nothing less than a first-round draft pick. But he's there for less than a week when Buffalo trades him, in October of 1976, to Houston, for *two* first-round picks. Moses is fortunate in that Houston's coach is Tom Nissalke, who had been Moses' first pro coach when he was with Utah in the ABA. Tom knows how to squeeze the maximum out of Moses.

By the time Moses blossoms and realizes his immense potential, the Rockets have deteriorated and grown old as a team. Moses is the whole show. The Rockets can win only when he has a surreal evening, and he has a lot of those. But he hungers, as does every great athlete, for a championship. All of the individual skills in the world become meaningless to those who possess them without an accompanying title. Even the most gifted of athletes always feels a gnawing lack of fulfillment until he is a member of a team that wins it all. In the Sixers, Moses saw his chance for such fulfillment.

But there were, of course, the usual questions when he came to Philly. Some argued that he was, in reality, a power forward masquerading as a center. Others contended that he could not fit in on a running team, that he had always played a half-court,

182

deliberate, set-it-up offense. And there was the usual conjecture about whether he could coexist with Doc, and vice versa.

It took less than the first month of the 1982-83 season for Moses' performance to put a forceful end to all the speculation. Yes, he could play the running game. Yes, he could go up against any center in the league and be dominant. Yes, he could play defense. There didn't, in short, seem to be much of anything Moses Malone couldn't do. And after all those seasons of sporadic, sputtering, uneven performances out of the pivot, the Sixers found themselves with a center who was worth 25 points and 15 rebounds on just an average night.

"The thing about him," said Billy Cunningham, "is his consistency. Moses just never has an off night."

Mostly what Moses Malone brought to the Sixers was a whole new attitude. Remember that this was a team that had been denied, cruelly, at every turn. Three times in six years it had reached the playoff finals only to stumble. There had been a subtle psychological erosion.

"When you lose in the finals," said Pat Riley in an astute piece of analysis, "it takes a tremendous toll. You lose a little bit of your basketball life. The Sixers had a lot of guys who had tasted nothing but pain, and that's bad. It can have a subconscious carry-over effect. Getting Moses was the best move they could have made. It rejuvenated them. They went out and said, 'With Moses, we're going to win it this year.' You could look at them and see they were more committed."

It was an evaluation that was seconded by Mo Cheeks, who noted: "When we got Moses, our minds changed right away. Having him was an important thing for us psychologically, just as important as what he brings us on the floor."

In early December the Sixers played the Lakers in LA. Moses ran wild against Kareem. The Sixers won, and three straight times in the fourth quarter Moses turned offensive rebounds into baskets. In past years, those would have been six lost points, and would have resulted in six LA points. After that game Julius Erving was asked to measure the impact of Moses Malone on the Sixers, asked how much Moses meant to the team. Doc grinned and said: "Oh, I'd say about $13.2 million. Spread over, say, six years."

Touché.

Moses Malone leads the League in rebounding, that crucial aspect of the game in which you retrieve missed shots. In fact, he had more rebounds for the Sixers than Darryl Dawkins and Caldwell Jones combined had captured the season before.

"Basically," says Moses, "I just goes to the rack."

Simple. Elemental. The way he plays. Moses, you see, has reduced rebounding to its simplest mathematical terms. He assumes that every shot taken in a game will be a miss, and consequently he positions himself to go after every rebound. Most players, being human after all, will go after seven of every 10 rebounds and feel that they have exerted themselves above and beyond the call of duty. Moses goes after all 10. And then the next 10. And the 10 after that. Most players talk about second and third effort; Moses has sixth and seventh effort. He will relentlessly tip-tip-tip the ball, playing volleyball with it on the boards until he either whips an outlet pass, goes back up for a basket, or gets fouled. He is relentless and he is indefatigable. And he never seems to become discouraged, at least not to the point of saying, "Well, I won't try for this one."

Moses tries for *every* one.

When he comes out of a game, which is infrequently, he walks slowly toward the bench, head down, in that familiar sloping body tilt of his. Moses leans forward as he walks, in the stance of a sailor leaning into a heavy wind and negotiating a slippery deck. He sits down, takes out his mouthpiece and tucks it inside his wristband, and his eyes never leave the action on the court. He doesn't scan the stands; nothing distracts him from the game. It is as though he wears invisible blinders. He studies the other players' moves, filing away weaknesses in his memory bank. And then when it is time for him to re-enter, he does so solemnly, his face fixed always in that stern scowl that is equal parts intimidation and concentration. Moses *looks* mean. He plays that way, too.

He was born a block away from the Virginia Avenue

playground in Petersburg. Before he was two, his father was gone, and Mary Malone found herself with her only child. She raised him with her will and what she could earn as a nurse's aide and from wrapping meat at a supermaket. Moses gravitated to that playground and to its dusty basketball court. Johnny Byrd, who runs the neighborhood confectionery one house away from the two-story flat in which Moses was raised, remembers: "I never noticed him much, except when I'd close up at night. It'd be 2, 2:30 in the morning, and I'd hear Moses bouncing a ball alone over on the courts." It was the only place where he really felt at home, felt comfortable. He had the talent for basketball, and he worked at it. But all the other things that go with stardom were not natural.

He was leery of the recruiters from the 250 colleges that chased after him. He is shy by nature and through all of their courting he became a sullen recluse, even hiding under beds and diving out back windows. He came to feel that everyone wanted a piece of him, and the only way he could handle the pulling and tugging at him was not to endure it. When he was playing in Utah, a Salt Lake City disc jockey called him "Mumbles Malone" in a barbed reference to his response to interviewers; that is, when he even consented to an interview, which was seldom. Even today he remains pretty much a loner. Oh, he will talk and joke with the other players, but never intimately. "Just as soon as you think he's opening up to you," says one Sixer, "he pulls back. 'Way back. He'll tell you something, and it's something that really means something to him. But then the next minute, he's back to the way he always is."

After that memorable double overtime win against the Celtics, Billy Cunningham had scanned the final boxscore. Moses had scored 28 points, snatched 19 rebounds, played all but two minutes of regulation and all 10 minutes of the two extra periods. "It was like," said Billy C, "he got stronger the longer he played." Moses, quizzed about his Herculean effort, just shrugged and said: "Wanted to win."

During the regular season, he refused all personal appearances, and granted almost no interviews. And yet, even though Moses keeps the blinds pulled down, every once in awhile we could

185

get a peek inside him.

There was, for example, the time the Sixers played in Milwaukee, and Moses, checking out of the hotel, gazed at his bill and told the desk clerk: "Just want to check out of my room. Don't want to buy no hotel."

And there was the time when someone asked him what he had done over the summer. "Swim-pool," Moses grunted. Oh, the man said, you built a swimming pool? "No," replied Moses. "Went swimmin', played pool."

But the Sixers did not acquire Moses to win any elocution contests. They were not interested in his oratory, only in how he massaged the backboards. And he did that. And the fans took to him at once. Never was his salary brought up by those in the seats who were paying it. Probably because they could see how much of himself Moses expends. He is a world-class sweater. One trip down the floor and his pores open like faucets and the sweat gushes out of him, splattering the court, droplets glistening on his goatee. Moses' salary figures out to something like $500 a minute, but to watch him at work is to realize how he seems determined to be deserving of it. It helps, of course, that his job involves what he likes most in life. Even in the summer, Moses plays basketball back home in Houston every day. He is never out of shape.

He brings a whole new dimension to the 76ers, and they rush out to a phenomenal start. Of their first 57 games, they win 50. Moses, Doc, Andrew Toney, who emerges this season as a complete player, and Mo Cheeks all make the All-Star team. There is talk of a record. Exactly one decade after they have compiled the worst record in history, 9-73, there is the delicious possibility that the Sixers will exactly reverse that and go 73-9. The alltime record for most wins in an NBA season is 69, set by the Lakers.

The Sixers appear headed for 70 wins anyway, but as they pile up a commanding lead in their division, they finally lose two games in succession, and the magic 70 begins to slip away. Billy Cunningham wisely begins to rest players. He is not the slightest bit interested in winning 70 games at the expense of taking a tired, injured team limping into the playoffs where they will be vulnerable.

They settle for 65 wins, only 17 losses. Only three teams in NBA history have ever won more games in one season.

Along the way, the team has fortified itself, knowing that to go into the playoffs with four rookies is too risky. You can get away with inexperience in the regular season, but not in the playoffs. The most immediate need is another forward, a veteran. Reggie Johnson, in his third season and playing with Kansas City, is available. He interests us. Joe Axelson, the GM of the Kings, tells me: "We're willing to move him." And I replied: "Fine, but no player swap. Cash only." Joe said the asking price was $150,000.

In the meantime, another name pops up: Clemon Johnson of Indiana. Reggie Johnson is a lean, willowly, finesse kind of player, and Clemon Johnson is 6-10, with some bulk and muscle, and a good rebounder. He looks like a nice insurance policy in the pivot, a good back-up for Moses. Too, he can play center and Moses can be moved, on occasion, to power forward. Both players clearly will make the Sixers a more versatile team. And both are available because they will become free agents the following year, and their current employers do not have the financial resources to get involved in high-stakes bidding. But Indiana's asking price for Clemon is staggering—$300,000 plus a first-round draft pick. We balked at that.

Before Christmas, we had opened up a spot on the roster by waiving Mitchell Anderson. We bought Reggie Johnson on February 15, 1983, and he would have his moments. That same day, which is the trading deadline, I called Bob Salyers, the Indiana GM, and asked him how he was coming in his efforts to move Clemon. He said things weren't going well. I said, "Well, if nothing works out, give me a call." That night, it's after 11, and I'm in bed and the phone rings. It's Bob Salyers. "You still intersted in Clemon Johnson?"

I put on an old robe and slippers and went down to the kitchen. We have a wall phone and I ended up on it for the next three hours. I called Harold Katz and said: "You won't believe this, but Clemon Johnson is obtainable." I had called the NBA office, just minutes before the midnight trading deadline, and asked for an extension. Then Harold and Billy and I talked in a conference call. Indiana is adamant in their desire to acquire Russ Schoene from us. Russ is not a factor now, but we wonder whether he could become one. In the meantime, Bob Salyers is becoming irritated waiting for us to decide, and finally, he slams down the phone. The NBA is, simultaneously, warning us that we've got one more minute to make a decision. At that precise moment, one of my children wakens from a nightmare, screaming. Just your typical day at the office. Anyway we call back Salyers and the upshot is that we get Clemon Johnson, too. Plus Reggie. Johnson and Johnson join the 76ers. Not a bad pair of Band-aids.

They help almost as soon as they arrive, especially Clemon, who is a high-percentage shooter and an effective shot-blocker. Billy starts experimenting with Moses and Clemon in the same lineup. Moses' minutes played are not quite as high as they were in Houston, but that is to his benefit as well as the Sixers'.

In one of his rare utterances to the media, Moses says: "It's never easy for Moses. Moses got to get out there every night and work hard."

There is no denying that he does that. If Wilt Chamberlain had worked as hard as Moses does every night, all those records he set would be even more unreachable. Similarly, if Moses had Wilt's natural physical gifts to go along with his own enormous desire and his capacity for work, he would own most of the record book.

The Sixers cruise down the stretch of the regular season. They shatter all the home attendance records. They compile the best record in the league. They leave the Celtics choking on their exhaust. They assure themselves of the first-round bye in the playoffs, and avoid the miniseries. And the scenario for almost every game is the same—down the stretch, Moses Malone simply takes over. It is as though he wills the Sixers not to lose. The crowds chant his name, and he plows ahead with that baleful glare, muscling, intimidating, driving the Sixers to win after win.

It is a dream season.

And then, with only four meaningless games remaining in it, Moses, who has fulfilled the most outrageous of expectations, becomes frighteningly mortal. He develops tendonitis in one knee. Dr. Clancy says it does not appear too serious, but advises that no chances be taken. Moses will miss the last week of the season. It is a rest he has earned. But not one that he relishes. He chafes at not being able to play those final four games. He has never gone this long in his life without playing basketball.

With the season concluded and with a week's wait before they start the playoffs, the Sixers return to Lancaster and a three-day camp. Billy wants to keep them sharp. When you are accustomed to playing three and four games a week for the better part of seven months, a week away from the game can be awfully disruptive, can throw timing and instincts and reflexes out of kilter.

It is pleasant to get back to Pennsylvania Dutch country as spring is unlocking the land, to savor such a successful season. But in the midst of all the congratulations and the anticipation of the playoffs, there is a moment of horror. Moses Malone's other knee is paining him.

He is rushed back to Philadelphia, and as he struggles to get out of the car, he almost collapses. He is barely able to walk.

This is like getting hit in the windpipe.

As he is carried away, his feet barely shuffling, there is an unspeakable dread. Has fate once more conspired to find a new way to thwart this star-crossed team?

You could almost hear the whirring of wings and the taunting cackles. Buzzard's luck one more time . . . .

13

Black Ties and Black Eyes

AT ITS BEST, professional basketball is high-speed ballet, orchestrated to the shrill *squeak-squeak* of sneakers, the thumping of bodies colliding at astonishing altitudes, the drumming rhythm of the ball pounding on the floor.

You take all of that and you add one more ingredient—passion—and you have the finest, fiercest, most ferocious, most enduring and endearing rivalry in all of professional sports.

Boston *vs.* Philadelphia.

The Celtics against the Sixers.

Every game is *Apocalypse Now*.

It is always the most eagerly anticipated game in the NBA. And, in contrast to many events in this age of hyperbole and oversell, it is never a disappointment. Philly and Boston always live up to our expectations. Indeed, it has been suggested that the NBA could do worse than eliminate the other 21 franchises and just let the Sixers and Celtics play each other 82 times a season. The problem with that, of course, is that none of the players would be ambulatory by Christmas. For what separates Boston-Philly from other games in a long, debilitating season, is that neither team ever

191

simply goes through the motions, neither takes a walking rest the nights they play each other.

There is no such thing, in this blood feud, as a "meaningless" game.

Each one is played with a snarling frenzy, bodies pinwheeling and splattering all over the arena, nerves frayed, tempers a raging fever. For the most part, they are clean games; it is just that emotions run so high that it's like broken beer bottles and brass knuckles in some back alley. If you designed an insignia for this rivalry, it would be a cocked fist.

A rivalry like this cannot be planned. It cannot be manufactured. It is something that has simmered, percolated, naturally evolved, and that is what gives it its charm.

It just sort of, well, happened. And now it feeds on itself, and no outside stimulus is required.

What makes a crackling good feud?

Well, repetition for one thing. And the Sixers and Celtics have all sorts of opportunities to go at each other every year. First off, they play once or twice every preseason, and those are anything but "exhibition" games. Then, under the current NBA schedule, they play each other six times during the regular season, three in Philly, three in Boston. (In earlier days, before expansion, they played more often than that.) And if they meet in the playoffs, which they have done 12 times since the 1957-58 season, they may meet as many as 15 times. In this case, familiarity does not breed contempt as much as it breeds a genuine grudge, tempered with a healthy respect.

Neither team is a mystery to the other. Each knows the other's plays, when they are apt to run them, and how. It all makes for good theater. Plus, the players themselves respond to the emotion of the moment. It is simply impossible to get "up" for every game over a seven-month season; but the players' juices are always at a bubbling froth for these games, and, consequently, the level of intensity is always high.

Another important factor in this Black Eye rivalry is the two cities. They have a lot in common beyond fairly close geographical

Doc drives against rookie sensation Dominique Wilkens of Atlanta in a 1983 game at the Spectrum.

This is what the Sixers got Moses Malone for—re-bounding. He led the league in retrieves, and in this shot, looks for an outlet pass against Milwaukee's Alton Lister and Charlie Criss in the 1983 playoffs.

Neither Doc nor Moses enjoys sitting during a game, but this moment is one to savor with trainer Al Domenico in the closing minutes of a Sixers' romp.

JOHN E. BIE

Harold Katz, the owner of the 76ers, has what he calls a "good money, bad money" business philosophy. He spent $13 million to acquire this player. It was most definitely "good money."

Billy Cunningham's least concern was that Moses Malone would be ready to play every night.

There are bigger players and faster players and players who can jump higher, but no one concentrates more intently, more relentlessly, than Moses.

MIKE MAICHER

Doc pauses before a crucial free throw ...
then cocks and fires...

The Doctor knifes between Clark Kellogg
and Brad Branson of Indiana in 1983 game.

In typical all-out fashion, Bobby Jones crashes for the ball against Boston in the 1980 playoffs. Julius Erving gets crunched while the Celtics' M. L. Carr and Larry Bird hope for a rebound.

JOHN E. BIEVER

Andrew Toney doing what he does best—leaving a defender off balance and helpless, in this case, Paul Mokeski of Milwaukee in the 1983 playoffs.

Doc throws down a two-handed thunderdunk while Detroit's Isaiah Thomas avoids the fall-out.

Rapidly improving Franklin Edwards pops a jumper over Milwaukee's Brian Winters in the 1983 playoffs.

Bobby Jones wrestles away a rebound from former Sixer Harvey Catchings of Milwaukee in the 1983 playoffs.

JOHN E. BIEVER

MIKE MAICH

Reggie Johnson (33) gets rebound position over Truck Robinson of the Knicks in a late season Spectrum tussle. Johnson was acquired from Kansas City for cash in February 1983 and helped the Sixers win several games with his offensive skills.

Billy Cunningham sends in the NBA's best sixth man.

The White Shadow drives for two against Edgar Jones of Detroit.

JOHN E. BIEV

One of the biggest steals in the 1978 NBA draft, Maurice Cheeks has helped erase the memories of Craig Raymond, Shaler Halimon, Al Henry, Dana Lewis, Fred Boyd and Marvin Barnes, all first-round Sixer picks who flopped.

Marc Iavaroni drives around Paul Pressey of Milwaukee in the 1983 playoffs.

Iavaroni hustled his way from obscurity in Italy to a starting spot on the 1983 world champions.

The February acquisition of Clemon Johnson (45) from Indiana provided the Sixers with depth and rebounding help for the championship drive. Marc Iavaroni watches CJ's balancing act.

IN E. BIEVER

In a mid-air meeting of NBA All-Stars, Moses Malone swats at Marques Johnson's long-range jumper in the 1983 playoffs.

Earl Cureton, who is now playing in Italy, provided inspiration in the Sixers' wipeout of Los Angeles in the 1983 finals.

Mark McNamara, the Sixers' No. 1 pick in 1982, buries an elbow in Mark Olberding of Chicago.

MIKE MAICHER

BILL HANZLIK

Clint Richardson, who was almost cut by the Sixers during training camp of his rookie season in 1979, has worked hard and has become one of the NBA's most valuable third guards.

The new world champions deplane in Philadelphia, with Billy Cunningham holding the trophy aloft. Mo Cheeks and Moses Malone precede him down the victory ramp. Jack McMahon and Mark McNamara celebrate in the background.

The Philadelphia sports fan has become legendary. After more than a decade of frustration, Sixers fanatics finally had a season to rejoice.

MAICHER

More than 55,000 fans turned out at Veterans Stadium at the conclusion of a wild victory parade. Owner Harold Katz shows them the trophy while Billy Cunningham acknowledges the adulation.

Doc, after seven years of pursuit, finally could signal that the Sixers were, indeed, No. 1. Marc Iavaroni agrees.

This is the official team photo...of the team that paid its long-standing debt.

proximity. They are alike in character and heritage. Each is proudly rooted in the American Revolution and each is a fascinating mix of the historical past and the melting pot present; each has its dwindling aristocracy and each has its own vibrancy. Boston has clam chowder and Paul Revere and the old North Church. Philadelphia has hot pretzels with mustard, Ben Franklin and the Liberty Bell.

Enough of culture. There is another similar tie between the two cities. Sports. They are probably the two best pro sports cities in America. Their fans are knowledgeable and vocal. And for several years now, their teams have been stunningly successful. Boston has the Bruins and Red Sox and Patriots . . . and the Celtics. Philadephia has the Flyers and Phillies and Eagles . . . and the 76ers. Most of them are usually contenders, and, very often in recent years, champions.

But what probably has made this rivalry so fascinating is its bizarre history. It is a rollcall of dramatic, unpredictable finishes, of one-point losses in seventh games, of losing at home when you were a mortal lock, of winning on the road when everyone else had buried you. There is an old saying in sports that the only sure thing is that there is no such thing as a sure thing, and nowhere is that quite as appropriate as it is in this rivalry.

Before the 1982-83 season, the Sixers and Celtics had met in the Eastern Conference finals for three straight springs. Philly won, 4 games to 1, in the spring of 1980. Boston won the following year, 4-3, in a Sixers collapse that is painful to recall because it featured the squandering of what looked like an insurmountable 3-1 lead in games, *plus* leads going into the stretch run of each of the last three games. Then, in the spring of '82, there was another memorable playoff, the Sixers winning in the seventh game, *at* Boston, when everyone had given up on them.

Philadephia's recent success in this series is important to understand because for such a long time this rivalry was so one-sided. In the 12 times the two have met in the playoffs, Boston leads, 8-4, but remember that the Celtics won the first five, and seven of the first eight. You can understand, then, the teeth-gnashing frustration that had built up in Philly. Boston was the perennial tormentor and Philadelphia the longsuffering victim.

This goes back to the beginning of the rivalry and is best personified in two players, the opposing centers: William Fenton Russell of Boston and Wilton Norman Chamberlain of Philadelphia, the best defensive player of all time against the best offensive player ever, each devastatingly dominant in his particular specialty.

It is the American trait to root for the underdog and thus you would have assumed that when Russell and the Celtics kept beating Chamberlain and Philadelphia that people might start pulling for Philly.

No way.

Perhaps it was because of his Olympian size, his Herculean strength, his scowling, stoic demeanor, but Wilt was somehow always perceived as the archvillain. Darth Vader in sneakers. He was always touted as the *individual* while Russell played with a *team*. The implication was that Wilt was selfish while Russell was selfless. Accurate or not, fair or not, it was the image that Wilt was saddled with early on and it proved to be as permanent as a vaccination scar.

Both men were extraordinarily tall in an age when 7-footers were glandular rarities, but because Wilt was a few inches taller, it was seen as an unfair advantage by many. Both men wore beards, but people interpreted Russell's goatee as charming while Wilt's was vaguely sinister. The deck was stacked against Wilt. He would get the points and the rebounds, Russell and Boston would get the title, and much of the public interpreted this only as justice served. If Wilt, and, by association, the team, wanted sympathy, they had to consult the dictionary to find it; they sure weren't going to get it from the country at large.

Chamberlain's rookie year, in the 1959-60 season, he averaged 37.6 points a game, and Philadelphia lost in the Eastern finals to Boston, 4 games to 2. It set the tone. And nobody mourned, except in Philly.

"No one," Wilt once sighed, "loves Goliath."

And, outside Philadelphia, hardly anybody rooted for

Goliath's team when it played Boston.

Just as cities are important in this rivalry, so are the personalities. Philly-Boston wouldn't be the same if the towns involved were—oh, say, Baltimore and Detroit. And this rivalry might never have blossomed into what it has were it not for the Chamberlain-Russell duels. Similarly, the rivalry has been nurtured by two stars who succeeded Russell and Chamberlain: Larry Bird for Boston, Julius Erving for Philadelphia. They have kept the heartbeat going, and each is accorded uncommon respect when he plays in the other's arena. You can almost sense the fans of Boston hoping Doc will have a big game, but in a losing cause. And the Philly fans, notorious for their booing, have awarded Bird warm receptions and generous applause.

"You hear a lot of talk about 'hate' in this series," Julius Erving reflected during last year's playoffs with Boston, "but I prefer to turn that around a little and say Boston always has been the team we love to beat the most. I don't hate the Celtics, I just love to beat them."

In the early days, when Boston was beating Philly like a drum in the playoffs, one other personality was central in planting the seeds.

Arnold (Red) Auerbach.

He was the coach of the Celtics in those days and an acknowledged tactical genius. Red also had this infuriating habit of firing up his victory cigar when the outcome was no longer in doubt. It was bad enough for Philadelphia fans to see their team going down to defeat against the despised Celtics, but then Red would reach for his stogie and start peeling off the cellophane very deliberately, with great relish, and this absolutely incensed the fans. Red was the portrait of arrogance in those moments. He had gloating down to a fine art. He was also belligerent, bellicose and capable of generating an amazing amount of animosity. Every time he lit one of those victory cigars, it was as gallingly painful to Philadelphia fans as if he had lit bamboo slivers under their fingernails.

Boston fans, of course, howled gleefully when the moment of

195

the cigar would arrive.

For Philadelphia, in the beginning of this feud, there was hardly ever a cigar. Usually, only the taste of ashes.

So you can imagine how sweet the vengeance in the spring of 1967, when the Sixers, for the first time after five consecutive eliminations from the playoffs by Boston, beat the Celtics. It was a wipeout. Four games to one, the final a 140-116 rout, in Philly.

It would be the spring of 1977 before Sixers fans would know such ecstasy again. But though there have been occasional lapses, the blood feud has never quieted.

We are into the third decade of this rivalry now, and it has spilled over into a number of battlegrounds—in the Arena, in Convention Hall, in the Palestra and in the Spectrum in Philadelphia; in the Arena and in the Garden in Boston; and its fires have enveloped an outpost or two along the way, including Hershey and Providence.

The sites of these wars are important because they have lent something, too; a certain ambiance. Call it waterfront-dive-tacky. But then if you're fighting a war, you need foxholes, and Boston-Philly is hardly drawing room genteel.

Boston Garden, where the Celts still play, will never make the cover of *House Beautiful* or *Better Homes and Gardens.* Its unique parquet floor is one of the most famous and familiar stages in sports. But what those people who watch on TV and who have never been there do not realize is the sleazy sort of charm the Garden possesses. It is located—actually, a first-time visitor needs a road map—in a rambling, ramshackle structure that is a train station. You can easily get lost in the bewildering labyrinth of corridors trying to find the Garden. There is a distinctive aroma, too, a not particularly appealing mixture of popcorn and a campout by the American Association of Winos.

But then the Convention Hall in Philadelphia was hardly La Scala, either. The Sixers long ago moved into the Spectrum, that circular building in South Philly that is a considerable step up. And yet there was something lost when they made that move, like holding a stag smoker at the Ritz instead of the American Legion

196

hall. Because there is a rawness, an earthiness, something charmingly base and bare-knuckled fundamental about Boston and Philly. It belongs in a dark, smoky arena where the air is thick and blue, where sunlight is foreign, where the atmosphere is coarse, not antiseptic.

Then again, the games are always so entertaining that you could play them on a polar ice cap and it would still be a full house. The Eskimos, who might not know a slam dunk from a kayak, would take one look at Philly-Boston and grunt their recognition. And approval. "Yes," they would say, "we have something similar to this up here. It's when two polar bears fight to the death."

The fans work themselves into a frenzy, too.

It is not a high society turnout. They are mostly blue-collar, hard-core hoops fans who come to these games. They come early—ringing the court, three- and four-deep during the warm-ups in Boston—and they stay late. And when the game is in Philly, they start congregating in clots outside the Spectrum long before the doors are opened.

And, once inside, they never sit on their hands.

"When we play in Philadelphia," said Kevin McHale of the Celts, "it sounds like the crowd has saved up their voices for three months just getting ready for us."

It's the same way in the Garden, the Celtic backers rolling out tidal waves of noise, trying to drown the Sixers, trying to surge their team to victory.

At the same time, one of the marvels of this rivalry is the genuine regard the fans have for the opposition. The best example was in the seventh game of the 1982 playoffs, in the Garden. When the game was inside the final two minutes and it was obvious that the Sixers would win, the Boston fans picked up a chant that became a rousing, ringing, rallying cry: "Beat LA . . . Beat LA . . . Beat LA!" The Lakers would be the Sixers' next opponent, and now the Celtics' fans, resigned to defeat, were uniting behind the team that had vanquished their team. It was a stirring sound, the epitome of sportsmanship. And the fact that the fans in Boston could swallow their disappointment and offer encouragement in

197

almost the same moment spoke volumes for the human spirit. For now, Boston would root for the Sixers.

But only until the next time the Celtics played Philadelphia.

The cast changes but the emotions build. Wilt, the Big Dipper, leaves and is succeeded by Julius, the Doctor. Hal Greer is gone from the Sixers, but Andrew Toney takes his place. Russell retires but Larry Bird comes on. John Havlicek is out, Kevin McHale is in. The Celtics' fans don't have Darryl Dawkins to boo any more, but they have decided that Moses Malone is an equally inviting target. Red Auerbach sits in the stands these days, but there are still diehard Philly fans who remember him . . . and yearn to offer him a light—if they can douse him with gasoline first, that is.

"I think," said Billy Cunningham, "the sweetest sound in all the world is playing in the Garden and getting so far ahead of them that you take the fans right out of the game. They just sit there. That silence is better than a standing ovation."

In recent years, another rivalry has budded and now bursts into full flower.

Philadelphia *vs.* Los Angeles.

The Sixers against the Lakers.

We are talking about different cities, about culture shock, about vastly different fans and a different style of basketball. But the passions, the obsessions, are still there.

They are just more subtle.

The savagery is more muted. The fists are still clenched, but they are swathed in velvet.

Lakers-Sixers games are more like 48-minute relay races, while Celtics-Sixers games tend to be more like rugby scrums.

If there is one team in the NBA that likes to run more than Philly, it's LA. The Lakers drink jet fuel instead of Gatorade. Their insignia should be a starter's pistol and a checkered flag. Even at rest, their engines are at high idle.

Which, of course, is precisely the style the Sixers favor. So it is a mirror matchup when they meet, each trying to run the other into the ground. With Boston and Philly, it's like wrist-wrestling in a bar, one trying to impose his will on the other. With LA and Philly, it's more a 100-yard dash, each trying to choke the other in his exhaust.

The feud doesn't have the long past and the rich tradition, but the Black Tie rivalry, especially over the last three years, has been every bit as meaningful as the Black Eye rivalry.

The Lakers play in the Western Division and as a result meet the Sixers only twice during the regular season. Nonetheless, it's still a sell-out when the other comes to town. And, of course, in the 1980, 1982, and 1983 championship finals, the Lakers and Sixers were the combatants.

And, like Boston in the beginning, Los Angeles has been the tormentor, Philadelphia the frustrated. The Lakers had won the first two times, both in the sixth game. Each time, the Sixers had gotten safely past Boston, had beaten an old bugaboo, and each time, before they could savor this revenge, they were knocked off by LA. So this spices the rivalry. This, and the knowledge that the only way the two teams ever can meet in the playoffs is for everything.

In other words, each game they play against each other is high stakes. Because you only meet twice in the regular season, you want to win both badly to set the tone . . . to set the tone just in case you go at it again for the championship.

If Boston-Philly is blue collar, then LA-Philly is ultrasuede. The Lakers play in the Forum. The *Fabulous* Forum, they like to call it. But when you're in the shadow of Hollywood, modesty is not a factor. The parking lot looks like a Mercedes-Benz showroom. Outside of a presidential inauguration, you'll never see more limousines in one place at one time. A Laker fan wears Gucci sneakers. He sips from a silver flask; Perrier, of course. He arrives fashionably late, with a cashmere demeanor. But once the ball goes up and the Sixers and Lakers start running, some of that California mellow leaves him. His carefully tanned face goes flush and, to his chagrin, he finds himself lurching to his feet, shaking his fist and bellowing.

But such uncool behavior is acceptable because, look, right

there in his season courtside seat, within arm's reach of Billy Cunningham, there's Jack Nicholson, and he's going berserk, screaming at the officials, winking at Kareem, standing to tell Magic to slow things down, get under control. Marquee names litter the audience. You can fill your autograph book at halftime. *One Flew Over the Cuckoo's Nest* might best describe the Boston-Philly rivalry, but it's LA-Philly that turns on Jack Nicholson.

And most everyone else, too.

The Lakers could only play in LA. They fit the town perfectly, their roster reflecting the Land of the Jacuzzi.

There's Kareem Abdul-Jabbar, 7 feet whatever; he has a bald spot, but no one is aware of it because it's on the very top of his head and to get up there you need a Sherpa guide and several oxygen tanks. He is marvelously graceful and fluid for his size, and he has the approximate wingspan of a 747. He is flowing and tall and has this regal, imperious look, and hardly ever gets ruffled.

There's Magic Johnson, with the piano keyboard smile, threading another impossible pass, doing something outrageous every game. It's always showtime with Magic.

There's Jamaal Wilkes. Silk, they call him. Is that perfect? Is that LA? He shoots a sort of corkscrew jumpshot that he unleashes from behind his ear. On anyone less physically eloquent, it would look awkward; on Silk, it looks charmingly eccentric. How smooth is he? Well, Paul Westhead, who used to coach him, said: "Silk is like snow falling off a bamboo leaf." Westhead, you should know, is a Shakespearean scholar.

Anyway, there are a lot more like those three. So the Lakers sort of resemble Swan Lake. Minus the tutus.

They soar and swoop and scorch. Naturally, Julius Erving is very big with the folks at the Forum. Doc does one of his wing walks and even the suavest holds his head and swoons. They would love to have Doc on the Lakers.

Their owner, Jerry Buss, could afford him. He owns the team, plus the Forum. And a lot of other things, too. Most of his little black book listings came right out of *Playboy*. Which reminds me that the Lakers also have a group of dancers that entertain during

200

timeouts. They're so gorgeous it makes you want to stick a fork in your leg.

So there tends to be a lot of flash and dash when the Lakers and Sixers go at it, a lot of sequins and sparkle. In the audience and on the court.

The Black Eye rivalry is older, nastier.

But the Black Tie rivalry is getting there.

Mostly, while professional basketball is a team sport, it is sold by individuals. People come out to see certain players rather than whole teams.

With a couple of very notable exceptons: Boston-Philly and LA-Philly.

These are big box office because, at this moment, the five biggest names in the NBA are Julius Erving, Moses Malone, Larry Bird, Magic Johnson and Kareem Abdul-Jabbar. And when it's the Black Tie and the Black Eye rivalry, then you get all five of them.

Now *that's* a full house any gambler would bet the mortgage on.

14

Deliverance

"FO' . . . FO' . . . FO'. . . ."

The words belonged to Moses Malone. You have to understand that Moses sometimes tends to speak as though he were sending a Western Union message and is being charged by the word. He is, at such moments, terse and blunt. He had spoken to the media rarely during the regular season, but as the playoffs wore on he became more talkative until, finally, he was downright garrulous at the end. "You come back tomorrow," he had told writers after Game 3 of the finals, "and I'll be here."

On the eve of the 1983 playoffs, Billy Cunningham had, kiddingly, asked Moses how he thought the 76ers would fare in the playoffs. Moses never hesitated. He barely looked up from unlacing his sneakers and said, in that rumbling basso voice: "Fo' . . . fo' . . . fo'. . . ."

Contained in that staccato litany was the cryptic suggestion that the Sixers would sweep every team they played. They would win the first four of the first series, then the first four of the next, and the first four of the finals. "Fo' . . . fo' . . . fo' . . . ." It was the most audacious sort of prediction. For one thing, it had never been done. No team had ever ripped through the playoffs without a single loss. In fact, since the inception of the playoffs format in which a team is required to win 12 games to take the title, the very best any of them had managed was to require 14 games to win 12. Even a gaudy 12-2 record had been accomplished only twice in history. And here was Moses blithely predicting 12-0. For another thing, there is a sort of unwritten code in sports that, for publication at least, a team is always cautious. You may feel utterly confident inside but you are supposed to exercise great care and temper any statements that might smack of optimism. But Moses obviously sensed something. He was brimming with confidence. Of course, his prediction got out and was repeated. Often. Moses couldn't have cared less. He stood by it. And it seemed to inspire the Sixers. They used it as a rallying point. "Fo' . . . fo' . . . fo' . . . " was the Sixers' battle cry.

As for Moses, he became not only a widely quoted phrasemaker but an astonishingly accurate prophet. The Sixers would fall only one game short of realizing the standard Moses had set for them.

What also made Moses' prediction seem so outrageous at the time was that he himself was hobbled. Remember that he had missed the final four games of the regular season with tendonitis in one knee, and then, after sitting and chafing for two weeks, he tried to return too hard and too soon, damaging the other knee during practice. When the Sixers began the playoffs, Moses Malone's knees were swathed in protective sleeves, and no one was sure whether he could make even one trip up and down the court. Indeed, there was a fog of despair over the Sixers as they prepared for the playoffs of 1983. There was the uneasy sensation that, somehow, they might be denied again.

But not this time. No, this time was to be the time of deliverance. This time, the Team of Torment would become basketball champions of the planet. And this is how they did it . . .

THE KNICKS

Sunday, April 24, 1983. The Spectrum. Game 1 of the NBA

quarterfinals. The 76ers against the New York Knicks. The game was almost four minutes old before the ball went inside to Moses. Billy Cunningham leaned forward in his seat in the expectant manner of an accused man on trial awaiting the jury's verdict. The rest of the Sixers stood, transfixed, waiting to see whether they had a gimpy-kneed question mark in the pivot. Malone wheeled, authoritatively, and surged through a defensive triple-team, pushing up a hook shot. The ball bounced on both sides of the rim, and fell through the nets. Billy exhaled mightily. Some of the Sixers sneaked grinning peeks at each other. The verdict was in: acquittal. Moses could play. He could play 38 minutes that afternoon and score 38 points and spear 17 rebounds, and the Sixers cruised, 112-102. The most meaningful statistic was that Moses had *zero* limps.

And while big Moses was savaging the Knicks inside, Little Mo was killing them softly from outside. Maurice Cheeks slithered through the Knicks' trapping defense and accounted for 34 points— the 14 he scored himself, plus the other 20 he set up with his passing.

"Moses has a very high threshold of pain," said trainer Al Domenico. "He could hardly walk when we drove him back from Lancaster. But the thing about him is his desire. Maybe if you cut off both his legs, that'd be the only way you'd keep him out of there. He's never won a championship and he really wants one."

Looking back on the entire playoffs, the turning point probably was this game. What if Moses' knees had given way? What if the Sixers would have had to play without him?

"When I saw my knees weren't going to hurt a whole lot," Moses said, smoothing the ice packs that were strapped to each one, "I told myself, 'Well, now, I might as well go ahead and play a little bit.'"

The Knicks didn't know it then, but they were dead. Their chances for an upset had melted, just like the ice bags that formed small puddles at Moses Malone's feet.

Wednesday, April 28, 1983. The Spectrum. Game 2. The Sixers were dead. Stone-cold stiff. Pennies-on-the-eyelids, pull-up-the-sheets, ready-for-planting dead. In the second minute of the second half, they trailed the Knicks by 20 points. Worse, they looked sluggish. The Knicks had succeeded in reducing this to a halfcourt slowdown. And then the Sixers unfurl what will become their trademark through these playoffs. "Comeback" is too tepid. This was Lazarus in sneakers. In one incendiary spurt, they outscore the Knicks 22-1. They ride that roll, and in 16 minutes score 40 points, their voracious defense holding New York to only 11. Instead of a crushing defeat, they win going away, 98-91. And they do it with a 10-man roster; Andrew Toney is sidelined with a deep thigh bruise and Bobby Jones is bed-ridden with the flu. So it's Moses and Mo again, Moses with 30, Maurice with 26.

"Even though it happened against us," said Knicks Coach Hubie Brown, admiringly, "what the Sixers did, it was beautiful to watch." And then Hubie tried hard for a psychological edge, suggesting that the Knicks had given the Sixers something to think about, the way they broke open the first half. "Sure, the Sixers went out and exploded on us in the third quarter. Okay, it happened. But it's over. But we still came out of it with a positive. I don't think they thought we could play that good. I feel that, in the playoffs, crushing defeats are only in the minds of the people who allow them to be crushing." He is whistling past the graveyard.

Saturday, April 30, 1983. Madison Square Garden, New York City. Game 3. Tie game. Four seconds left. Franklin Edwards finds himself with the basketball. Instincts take over. He darts around his defender, the stronger but slower Ernie Grunfeld. So Truck Robinson trundles over to intercept him. Franklin pump-fakes and Robinson bites. He jumps to block the shot. Edwards waits. As Truck comes down, Franklin goes up, releases a jump, leaning in, from maybe 10 feet away. He banks it delicately off the glass, with the clock two seconds from expiration. Final: Philadelphia 107, New York 105. Franklin Edwards was in the game at crunch time because Andrew Toney's thigh had tightened up. So Franklin Delano Edwards, from Harlem, lived out a fantasy in the very same building where he had first dreamed. "I remember," he said, "me and some friends used to come down to the Garden on the Seventh Avenue subway and get seats all the way up top. Then, when all the people had left in the last couple of minutes, we'd sneak down and sit in the seats close to the floor. Then, after the games, my friends and I used to run out on the court, and the ushers would chase us." Now he was being pursued again—by writers and photographers and TV cameras. "You can sure see the game a lot better from down here," says Franklin Edwards, grinning.

Sunday, May 1, 1983. The Garden. Game 4. This is May Day for the Knicks, but no matter how many frantic SOS's they tap out, nothing can save them. To their credit, the Knicks have risen to a higher level in this series, played beyond their capabilities. But it isn't enough. This one is close until the final seven minutes. Rory Sparrow drives for a layup and a Knicks lead, but Moses swats away the shot to Franklin Edwards. In turn, Edwards passes to a flying Julius Erving, who swoops, stuffs, is fouled, and makes the free throw. Moses takes over from there. He rebounds, he scores, he rejects. Eight days earlier, he was believed to be one short step away from the Mayo Clinic. Or Lourdes. Instead, in a four-straight sweep, Moses scores 125 points, seizes 62 rebounds. "If he's hurting," said Truck Robinson of Moses, "then I'd sure like to see him when he's well." The sweep buys the Sixers a week's worth of rest. It is welcome because they are in desperate need of some whirlpool time, some mending and healing.

THE BUCKS

It was supposed to be Boston. It was supposed to be the Black Eye rivalry flaming anew. But the Celtics aren't here this spring. They have been eliminated in the quarterfinals by Milwaukee. Not just beaten, but humiliated. They are swept and left in tattered disarray, yelping at each other and at their coach, Bill Fitch, who will eventually quit. That the 76ers and the Celtics will not be meeting in the playoffs is regarded in some quarters as having a World War without Germany. The Bucks instead of the Celtics?

207

There are some who feel this is like getting Miss Piggy when you were expecting Bo Derek.

Actually, while a lot of people weren't noticing, the Bucks and Sixers have been firing up a nasty little squabble of their own. This is the third straight year they have met in the playoffs. In 1981, it went the seven-game limit, came down to the last shot, and ended with the Sixers surviving by a single point. In 1982, the Sixers prevailed again, but needed six games. And, over the last three regular seasons, the Bucks and Sixers have played each other 17 times, Philly holding a slim 9-8 advantage. They have played three overtimes, with 11 games decided by three points or less. Good enemies are hard to find, but the Bucks are a worthy replacement for the Celts.

Sunday, May 8, 1983. Game 1, NBA semifinals. The Spectrum. The Sixers steal this one. Literally. It has gone into overtime and the Bucks are ahead, 109-108, with 1 minute, 36 seconds to play. Clint Richardson has just scored for the Sixers, depositing two free throws. Alton Lister throws an inbound pass to Sidney Moncrief. But The White Shadow is there. Bobby Jones plucks the ball away as he is leaping. He pirouettes in midair and feeds a soft, accurate pass to Clint, who is under the basket. Clint stuffs. The Sixers have the lead and they hang onto it, 111-109. Clint scores all seven Sixers points in the overtime. "I'm sure Milwaukee didn't expect me to do that," he says. "I don't imagine anyone in the building expected it. Obviously, Bobby turned it around with that steal. I'd just made those two free throws and then drifted down towards the baseline to pick up Moncrief. I wanted to play him fullcourt defense, Next thing I know, the ball is in my hands. Bobby saw me even while he was twisting in midair. Fed it perfectly. But that's just Bobby Jones. He seems to make those plays all the time." Clint was in the game because Andrew Toney had fouled out. This is the second time in five games that the Sixers have been bailed out by their bench: Franklin Edwards in the Garden against the Knicks, now Clint. "Most of our bench could start someplace else," he says. "You'd better be confident in the clutch here, or they'll get someone else. I like to think that I'm a starter who just doesn't happen to start."

Wednesday, May 11, 1983. The Spectrum. Game 1. This is a savage scrum, a defensive purist's delight. It is broken open by Moses Malone, who scores 26 points as the Sixers win a grind-it-out wrestling match, 87-81. Billy Cunningham and Don Nelson conduct a coaching clinic, a cerebral battle of thrust, parry and counter, orchestrated to the background music of thudding bodies and crunching collisions. The teams have played each other so often over the last three years that they are intimately familiar with each other's tactics. "I guess it's obvious Don and I are testing the rules with all the offensive variations we're trying," says Billy. "But both teams are so good defensively that you have to keep searching for alternatives." There is almost an ugly moment when Andrew Toney careens in for a layup and big Bob Lanier tries to stop him. Lanier grabs at Andrew, but his forearm clotheslines Andrew's windpipe. For one frightening moment, decapitation seems possible. But Lanier grabs Andrew with his other arm to prevent a nasty spill. Billy rushes to the scene, barking at Bob Lanier, and Lanier snaps back. Billy's contention is that Lanier could have reached for a less vulnerable portion of Andrew's anatomy. Lanier, of course, is roundly booed every time he touches the ball thereafter. It is an emotional series for Bob Lanier, who has played 14 years without winning a title. He has said this will probably be his last try. The Sixers are off to a 2-0 lead and haven't lost a playoff game yet. There is one disquieting note: Julius Erving. Doc has been struggling with his shooting, and his knees are bothering him. Billy professes to be unconcerned: "He'll come around. We've been winning even though he hasn't been scoring like he can, but you just know he'll explode. That's the beauty of Doc." In the midst of all this, one rather imposing statistic surfaces, a statistic that emphatically proves how the Sixers have developed a killer instinct. During the regular season, in 58 games they held the lead going into the fourth quarter. They won 56 of those games. And their record in the playoffs in similar circumstances is 5-0. Clearly, they are finishing what they start.

Saturday, May 14, 1983. Milwaukee Arena. Game 3. The Sixers prove rather conclusively that it is not necessary for them to be ahead going into the fourth quarter. This time they are behind by seven points. No matter. They hit the Bucks with a 33-point blitz and cruise in, 104-96. And Billy C is right; Doc does indeed erupt. He scores 26. Maurice and Moses help dominate, but it is Doc who has the crowd howling. This game becomes one of those open-court, end-to-end track meets, the kind of game in which Doc has always thrived. So he gives them his whole Flying Wallenda routine. It is as though he is answering the critics who have been wondering, out loud, if Doc is no longer capable of taking over a game. His performance, however, has to speak for itself. Because Doc, uncharacteristically, bolts from the locker room, returning to the team's hotel, which is only a block away, for a shower and change. To writers scurrying up the exit ramp after him, he says only: "I'll be back." What he neglects to add is that he means he'll be back for Game 4 tomorrow. "Any questions about Julius Erving were all answered today," says Billy, puffing contentedly on a victory cigar. "I thought Doc just played dynamite. Maybe we weren't getting him the ball enough, or in the right position. I do think his knees are sore. When you're that age (33) and you've played this game that long (12 seasons) something always aches. But we were 6-0 in the playoffs while he was struggling with his scoring, and that was just an added plus. Now he's back in the groove and we're 7-0."

Sunday May 15, 1983. Milwaukee. Game 4. No one knows it at the time but this is an historic game. It is the only one the 76ers will lose in these playoffs. Final score: Milwaukee 100, Philadelphia 94. The Sixers had been finding so many ways to win that you have begun to suspect they might never lose. For only the third time in 64 games, the Sixers fail to hold a fourth-quarter lead. They go a full four minutes without a point and are outscored in the final 5:42 by 15-6. "We didn't turn the screws defensively," says Billy. "We've been winning every close game with our defense, but today we allowed them some key offensive rebounds. But, hey, give them some credit. That's a good team." Yes, it is. The Bucks, like the

Knicks, have seen the Sixers bring out the best in them. Bob Lanier, in retrospect, plays Moses better than any other center, leaning on him with 265 pounds and 14 years of guile and experience. And the Bucks, this game, get a big contribution from Charlie Criss, who, at 5 feet, 8 inches, is the smallest player in the NBA. "Charlie," says Don Nelson, "has got a heart as big as Bob Lanier's feet." Don is a sleepy-eyed, rumple-faced realist. He has been involved in too many playoffs, as combatant and coach, to think that being down 3-1 is much better than being down 3-0. "I won't try to kid you," he agrees. "We're still in a big hole. But I am encouraged because I think today I finally discovered a secret for beating the Sixers." Everyone leans forward intently. "I wore my lucky green jacket," he explains. Well, so much for state secrets. Everyone knows its going to take something more potent than a wardrobe change. The Sixers, except for Maurice and Clint, have all left the locker room early. But none of them seem particularly distraught over their first playoff loss. "Last year," notes Clint Richardson, "it took us 14 games to get this far. This year, we've done it in only eight. And, besides, I didn't think we were going to keep on winning forever." For a while there, though, it seemed they might. It didn't take them long to regain the knack, however.

Wednesday, May 18, 1983. The Spectrum. Game 5. To their everlasting credit, the Bucks die hard. The 76ers jump to a 12-point lead. The Bucks whittle seven points off it. The Sixers do it a third time, up by 12. The Bucks finally have nothing left. The Sixers are splendid. Andrew Toney, his thigh healing, hits his first six shots on the way to 30 points. Moses adds 28, Doc 24, and Clint Richardson again suffocates Sidney Moncrief on defense. The Sixers win, 115-103. "They're better than us; that's the hard, cold fact," says Bob Lanier. "We knew we'd have to play superior basketball, and we did. But that still wasn't enough. Everybody on this team reached back and gave everything they could give. But when all is said and done, we got our butts kicked." Don Nelson is a believer in the Sixers. He flatly predicts a title. "This is the best team I've seen in ten years," he says. "They are the next world champions, in my opinion. They play a different style in the West, but I just can't see any team touching the Sixers. They have everything. There's not a missing link. There's not a weakness." And so the Sixers qualify for the finals again. It is the second straight year. It is the third time in four years. It is the fourth time since 1977. No other team has managed such success, such consistency. It is left to Julius Erving to put into words the challenge they now face: "We have the best team in basketball. Now all we have to do is go out and prove it."

THE LAKERS

In the final seven minutes of the last game against Milwaukee, the frenzied, sold-out Spectrum crowd has begun its chant: "We want LA . . . we want LA . . . ." It was a lusty, thundering roar, one of defiance, one born of the frustration of the springs of 1980 and 1982, when the Lakers had beaten the Sixers for the championship, each time in six games. The people were getting their wish. The Sixers would face the Lakers for the third time in four years. But it hadn't been all that easy for LA. Their outstanding rookie, James Worthy, was out with a broken leg. Bob McAdoo was slowed by a pulled thigh muscle. And San Antonio had pushed the Lakers in the Western semifinals. Strangely, the Spurs could win at the Forum, but couldn't win on their own court. They finally succumbed to the Lakers, in six games, but that last one LA had won by only one point, and the Spurs had squeezed off two shots in the closing seconds.

So the Lakers lined up for their third playoff game in less than five days. Still, they were the defending champions. And McAdoo was playing again. And there was still Kareem in the middle. And Magic. And Silk. And Norm Nixon. And Michael Cooper and Kurt Rambis. And there was that Lakers' confidence, buttressed by the knowledge that they had beaten these Sixers twice before in the playoffs. So it was not exactly an impoverished team that flew into Philadelphia. They had the champion's aura about them.

Sunday, May 22, 1983. The Spectrum. Game 1 of the NBA

finals. They almost let this one slip away. The Sixers look shaky down the stretch. With 1 minute, 44 seconds to play, they are ahead by eight. But in their next four possessions, a time for running out the clock, they turn the ball over three times, and they miss two free throws. But Julius Erving and Bobby Jones combine for a key rebound, and then Moses Malone buries a pair of insurance free throws and sucks up every missed LA shot. Final: Philadelphia 113, Los Angeles 107. "We did not play well at all," says Billy C. "It wasn't easy; not by any means," seconds Maurice Cheeks. Clint Richardson has another big game off the bench, scoring 15 points in the second half. "We know that LA is a lot more explosive than Milwaukee," he says, trying to explain why the Sixers lost an early 12-point lead. "You can't afford a lapse against the Lakers. But we pulled this one out and that was a key. If we had lost, we would have been in a hole and they would have been riding high. Now we know we can hang on." It is a brutal game. Andrew Toney and Norm Nixon collide chasing the ball, and both have to be helped off. They return, however, Nixon scoring 26, Toney 25. The difference, however, is in the middle. Moses outscores Kareem, 27-20, and, more importantly, out-rebounds him by a whopping 18-4. And in the second half, Kareem gets *zero* rebounds. It is to become a central theme throughout this series: Moses growing stronger as each game goes along, Kareem fading and tiring. The Lakers are content to chalk this one up to fatigue, and let it go at that. "We ran out of gas a little bit in the second half," says Kareem, shrugging. "It was a carry-over from a tough game against San Antonio the night before." For now, it is an acceptable excuse. But, very soon, the Lakers will exhaust every alibi.

Thursday, May 26, 1983. The Spectrum. Game 2. This is the one in which the Sixers discover they can win with Moses riding the bench. It is the discovery that will boost their confidence to a new plateau, and make them champions. Moses plays only 31 minutes, forced to sit because of foul trouble. It is not that he is not a factor, for he still scores 24, has a dozen rebounds. But in a critical five-and-a-half-minute stretch of the fourth quarter, he is out of the game. When he departs, the Sixers are ahead by four points. When he returns, they have doubled that lead. They are ahead, 95-87, with 2:24 left. They go on to win by 10, 103-93. Clemon Johnson is sick and help comes from an all-but-forgotten source: Earl Cureton. The Twirl scores only one basket, but its emotional impact is shattering. It is a Kareem-like sky-hook, and it is delivered *over* Jabbar himself. The key is that, with Moses out, the Lakers become a one-dimensional team on offense. Each trip down the court, they go to Kareem in the middle, again and again, trying to capitalize on the size mismatch. The result is that LA's offense becomes predictable. Bobby Jones, Maurice Cheeks, Julius Erving and Andrew Toney, anticipating the Lakers' strategy, collapse around Kareem and swipe the Lakers' attempted passes to him. Their defense, in turn, gets them doing what they do best, which is run. Andrew throws down a running lefthand hook. Mo lofts in a moonball. Bobby converts an offensive rebound and comes back with a two-handed thunderdunk off Doc's quick feed. "I feel like I do a lot of little things that aggravate him," says Earl, explaining how he defends against Kareem. "I push him around. I front him. I try to bother him." The most bothered person at this point is Pat Riley. The Lakers' coach surveys the final boxscore and sees some discrepancies that infuriate him. LA has been whistled for 29 fouls, the Sixers for 16. The Sixers have made 23 free throws, the Lakers three. The Lakers have set a record for fewest free throws attempted and made in a playoff game. Later, Riley singles out referee Darell Garretson for his ire, claiming that of 16 personals called by Garretson, 15 were against the Lakers. Riley will get a $3,000 fine for "questioning the integrity" of the officials. He calls it "chump change." But this time, as the series moves cross country, it is the other team that finds itself in unaccustomed retreat. This time, the Sixers are doing the pushing. This time it is the other team whose lips are whitened and tightened, whose eyes are crinkled with concern. "The Lakers," says Clint Richardson, "they've always been supremely confident, almost arrogant, when they've played us. It was like they just knew they could handle us when it really mattered. Now I think you can see it in their eyes; they're a little surprised that when they shove, we shove back."

Sunday, May 29, 1983. The Forum. Los Angeles. Game 3. It is inevitable after this one. The 76ers are going to win an NBA title now, and they know it, and now the Lakers know it, too. The Lakers, playing out of desperation, surge to a 15-point lead in the second quarter. In other years, the Sixers might have folded then and been routed. But there is a starch in their spines now. They chip away, go in at the half down by three points, and they are told by Jack McMahon: "You've seen LA's best shot. They can't play any better. You're only down three, and that's encouraging." It is tied at 72 after three quarters, and then the Sixers go on a rampage. They tear off a 14-0 run and they rip out the Lakers' jugular, 111-94. Doc and Andrew score 21 apiece. Bobby Jones, who has lost nine pounds fighting strep throat, adds 17. Mo Cheeks has four steals. And Moses is awesome: 12 points in the fourth quarter alone, 18 in the second half, 28 in all. Plus 19 rebounds. And a team high 6 assists. For the third straight game, the Sixers have overcome an LA halftime lead. The Lakers have run out of excuses and tactics. They have tried to contain Moses by using Kurt Rambis and Mark Landsberger as a tag-team defense. "Ain't no 6-8 player gonna check me," says Moses. "When I get the ball down low, it's all over." Rambis, changing clothes, puts on a T-shirt. On the front of it are stitched two large paw prints. "Those belong to Moses?" he is asked. "Nah," he replies. "They're too small. Besides, if they were Moses', they'd be all over my back."

The Sixers have become second-half killers, and with each game they are destroying the Lakers. They outscore them in the second half by nine points in Game 1, by 14 in Game 2, by 20 in Game 3. Moses Malone owns the fourth quarter. Billy says: "We want LA in four. We want people to remember this team." So this will be for revenge now. For atonement. For retribution. Billy can sense that the monkey is about to be dislodged from the Sixers' backs at last. But it is not just enough to shake that monkey. He wants to rip it off, slam it to the ground, trample it in the dust. The Sixers, to this point, are remembered for failures. Now he wants them to be remembered from an historical perspective, for not just winning a championship, but for doing it quicker, more efficiently than any other team. "We just like a little train," says Moses. "We got the momentum goin' now."

Tuesday, May 31, 1983. The Forum. LA. Game 4. At precisely 11:46 P.M., Eastern Daylight Time, the 76ers reach the rainbow's end. Deliverance arrives on a California evening thick with smog and laden with misty skies. The 76ers are free at last, free from the galling mockery of "We Owe You One." This is no longer a team for derision, but a team for the book. The record book. Final: Philadelphia 115, Los Angeles 108. A sweep. Incredibly, almost exactly the way Moses Malone had called it. It turned out to be "fo' . . . five . . . fo' . . . ." But that was close enough. They are behind, as usual, this time by 16, in the second half. It does not matter. They outscore the Lakers by 64-43 in the second half. The fourth quarter is even more lopsided, the Sixers winning the last 12 minutes by a convincing 33-15. The team that once swooned in the stretch now comes thundering home, trampling anything in its way. There is poetic justice in this one: Julius Erving scores 7 straight points during the Sixers' climactic closing surge. Doc recalls that in this same locker room, one year ago, he had wept for only the second time in his life. Now those are not tears cascading down his cheeks, but champagne. The wine of sweet, sweet retribution. Doc, remember, is the lone player left from the 1977 playoffs. This has been, more than anyone else's, his quest. Now, it is at an end at last. "Seven years is a long time," he reflects. And then, holding that golden trophy, he grins hugely and adds: "But it was worth the wait." The Sixers' locker room is chaos, geysers of champagne spewing everywhere. Moses is the MVP of the playoffs. It is a unanimous choice. In this game, the last one, he has scored 24 points and inhaled 23 rebounds. Earl Cureton introduces Moses to some friends by saying: "This is Al Capone Malone. He steals basketball games." Moses still has his uniform on, and, as always, it is soaked with sweat. Incongruously, he also has a tie knotted around his neck. He is the hardest working player in the league, perhaps in all of sports. He has infused this team with his relentlessness, his fourth-quarter savagery. All through the season, all through the playoffs, it seems there was always a period in the game, usually with about eight minutes left, when Moses would say: "This is *my* basketball. This is *my* game. Get out of my way!" There emerges, in this moment of celebration, a new Moses. He is almost childlike in his glee. And he seems happiest for one player—for Doc. "This is Doc's team," he says, "not Moses' team. Moses is just here to help him win. Moses is just a player, that's all Moses is." Amen to that. It is also a glorious triumph for Billy Cunningham, who has completed a coaching masterstroke. He has taken a team of individual offensive talent and remade it in his image—sacrificial, selfless—and molded them into a devastating defensive unit. "This is a team of stars," he agrees, "but they are stars who are willing to work on defense." Pat Riley knows there are no excuses left now—not fatigue, not injuries, not officiating. "The Sixers just never let up," he says. "They were always able to take their aggressiveness up to another level. Their disposition to dominate was better than ours." This team has played 95 games, counting the regular season and the playoffs. It has lost only 18 times. Moses grabs Billy C, who, it is rumored, may be quitting, and Moses says to him: "You gotta come back 'cause we're gonna repeat . . . and 'peat and 'peat and 'peat." It has a nice ring to it. Almost as catchy as "fo' . . . fo' . . . fo' . . . ."

THE PARADE

They rode on a flatbed truck with glass walls, but for them it was a chariot of gold. It bore them through a howling, shrieking wall of noise, through avenues of flesh and forests of index fingers and showers of confetti and thunderclaps of adoration from a city drunk on the ecstasy of a world championship.

The Sixers' victory parade began at 11:30 A.M., Thursday, June 2, 1983, in Center City, at 20th and JFK Boulevard. It wound through the heart of the business district, then down South Broad Street, ending up at Veterans Stadium. The crowd estimates along the route ranged from 500,000 to 1.7 million. There were another

217

55,000 waiting in the Stadium. It had been a sodden, soggy spring, but this day, almost prophetically, the sun shone bright and hot. The people cheered and waved in a berserk outpouring of affection. They rejoiced most of all for Julius Erving, who told them:

"To get where we're at today, we had to go through a whole lot more than four, five, four. But that's what happened in the script, and we love it. Four games, five games . . . we all wish it was that easy, but we all know it wasn't, not for us, not for you, and it never will be for anybody to get where we are today. I've been trying to get here for seven years. So let us take a moment and trace back a little way. On three different occasions, we almost made it. But those occasions should not be forgotten, because it wasn't just the 76ers that made it, it was the city of Philadelphia, too. After six years of knocking at the door, we went out and got ourselves a cast of hardhats, and we got the final piece of the puzzle [Moses], that made us complete in every sense of the word. There was nothing pretty about what we did to the NBA this year . . . it was *beautiful!* We thank you from the bottom of our hearts for this day, when you came out here with all of us to share what we all have worked so very hard for. And we're not going to let anybody take our title away."

It was a perfect summation, and it was typical of Doc that he would remind everyone that there was something gained from all those past frustrations, that there were positives to be gleaned from the negatives, if one only had the right perspective. Doc had handled himself with such dignity and grace in past defeats, and now he was a gracious winner as well. As the crowd roared, Doc triumphantly held aloft the golden championship trophy in one huge hand. With the other, he reached down and pulled Billy Cunningham to him, and they embraced. When they stepped back, their eyes filled with mist.

They were Rainbow Chasers no more.

The crusade had ended at last.

In Triumph.

Epilogue

L.A. made excuses,
    yes, the Lakers alibied,
so get the rice and rings ready, Philly,
    we're no longer bridesmaids,
    get set to meet the bride!
There was no June swoon this year,
    the Sixers found a better way,
let the Lakers croon the losers' tune,
    we swept 'em up in May!
Bobby did better than Bob McAdid,
    Clint stretched those spiderlike arms,
while Magic disappeared or hid,
    Maurice Cheeked and sneaked
and pilfered balls away,
    Earl found the cure in Number Two,
and Mad Andrew bombed away.
    Marc Iavaroni rumpled Rambis curtly,
as he swept the boards
    and threw outlets so expertly.
The Doctor soared and scored
    with his customary flair,
leaving Cooper in a stupor
    and the Silk grabbing in despair.

Prophet Moses came close to calling it
    when he said "Fo' . . . fo' . . . fo'."
Kareem puffed and huffed and cried,
    "Let me alone, Malone,
I can't take this anymo'."
    so the broom at the top completed
a sweet sweep of four,
    and the bottom line is, Sixers fans,
we don't owe you anymore.

We've cut through all the Lakers' alibis and bull,
and from this team to our faithful Sixer fans
    we say, "Paid in full!"
Pat Williams and Ken Hussar